INDEPENDENT SECTOR

INDEPENDENT SECTOR is a coalition of 750 corporations, foundations, and voluntary organizations with national interests in and impact on philanthropy, voluntary action, and other activities related to the educational, scientific, cultural, and religious life, as well as the health and welfare, of the nation.

INDEPENDENT SECTOR is a meeting ground where diverse elements in and related to the sector can come together and learn how to improve their performance and effectiveness.

INDEPENDENT SECTOR is serving the sector through
- education, to improve the public's understanding of the independent sector
- research, to develop a comprehensive store of knowledge about the sector
- government relations, to coordinate the multitude of interconnections between the sector and the various levels of government
- encouragement of effective sector leadership and management, to maximize service to individuals and society, by promoting educational programs for managers and practitioners
- communication within the sector, to identify shared problems and opportunities

The impact of INDEPENDENT SECTOR's effort can be measured by the growth in support of the sector, as manifested by increased giving and volunteering.

For additional information, please contact

INDEPENDENT
SECTOR

1828 L Street, N.W.
Washington, DC 20036
(202) 223-8100

PROFILES
OF
EXCELLENCE

E. B. Knauft
Renee A. Berger
Sandra T. Gray

PROFILES
OF
EXCELLENCE

Achieving Success
in the Nonprofit Sector

Jossey-Bass Publishers
San Francisco • Oxford • 1991

PROFILES OF EXCELLENCE
Achieving Success in the Nonprofit Sector
by E. B. Knauft, Renee A. Berger, and Sandra T. Gray

Copyright © 1991 by: Jossey-Bass Inc., Publishers
350 Sansome Street
San Francisco, California 94104
&
Jossey-Bass Limited
Headington Hill Hall
Oxford OX3 0BW

Copyright under International, Pan American, and
Universal Copyright Conventions. All rights
reserved. No part of this book may be reproduced
in any form — except for brief quotation (not to
exceed 1,000 words) in a review or professional
work — without permission in writing from the publishers.

Library of Congress Cataloging-in-Publication Data

Knauft, E. B. (E. Burt)
    Profiles of excellence : achieving success in the nonprofit sector
/ E.B. Knauft, Renee A. Berger, Sandra T. Gray.
        p.   cm. — (The Jossey-Bass nonprofit sector series)
    Includes bibliographical references and index.
    ISBN 1-55542-337-X
    1. Corporations, Nonprofit — Management.   2. Excellence.
3. Organizational effectiveness.   4. Corporations, Nonprofit — United
States — Case studies.   I. Berger, Renee A.   II. Gray, Sandra T.
III. Title.   IV. Series.
HD62.6.K56   1991
658'.048 — dc20   90-23637
                                                                          CIP

Manufactured in the United States of America

The paper in this book meets the guidelines for
permanence and durability of the Committee on
Production Guidelines for Book Longevity of
the Council on Library Resources.

JACKET DESIGN BY WILLI BAUM

FIRST EDITION

Code 9140

INDEPENDENT
SECTOR

A Publication of INDEPENDENT SECTOR

The Jossey-Bass
Nonprofit Sector
Series

LINCOLN CHRISTIAN COLLEGE AND SEMINARY

83603

Contents

ix

Contents

Foreword

The Organizing Committee which created INDEPENDENT SECTOR realized that any group dedicated to preserving and strengthening this unique side of America had to devote part of its effort to the "encouragement of effective leadership and management of philanthropic and voluntary organizations to maximize their capacity to serve society." Early in the new organization's life, a standing committee was established to pursue that charge. From the start, this committee was handicapped by limited literature and even general agreement about what constitutes excellence in nonprofit endeavor. The closest thing to a consensus was the view of many business people that voluntary organizations generally are poorly managed.

One of the frustrations for business people who serve on voluntary boards is that it is so hard to define and measure success. Nonprofits just don't have the simple pleasure of corporate bottom-line profits. Many businessmen and women want so desperately for voluntary organizations to mirror what they know best that they are extremely impatient with their nonprofit counterparts.

It has become routine to hear such observations as, "these do-gooders and bleeding-hearts just don't know how to manage" or "if we could just get more management discipline into these cause-oriented organizations, they would be far more effective."

It's my own observation that these perceptions are usually inaccurate and unfair. Voluntary organizations, like businesses and other human institutions, vary in their effectiveness. About one-third are models of excellence—beautiful examples of caring, innovation, and efficiency. One-third are average—good to fair—and one-third are poorly managed and generally ineffective.

Senator Robert Packwood, who chaired the Senate Commerce and Finance Committees and has had a good opportunity to observe all three sectors, says that on the basis of his regular dealings with government, business, and nonprofits, he finds that foundations and voluntary organizations are by far the most reliable—that is, they're most certain to do what they were established to do and what society expects of them. Andrew Heiskell, former chief executive officer of Time, Inc. and leader of many major nonprofit institutions, including some of the magnitude of Harvard University and others as small as local parks, has come to believe that "voluntary organizations demand much more of themselves than most businesses, and they get much more out of their boards, staff, and dollars."

In the March 1989 issue of the Conference Board's *Across the Board* magazine, Peter Drucker was asked, "Can you give . . . an example of a nonprofit organization that you consider well run?" He responded, "I am going to shock you. I don't know a single business that is nearly as well run as some of the well-run nonprofits. Nor as tough, nor as disciplined, nor as ruthless." For examples, he gave the Girl Scouts, American Heart Association, American Red Cross, Salvation Army, and even many "local pastoral charities." He explained that the complexities of working with diverse boards, fund raising, and broad social missions contribute to making these organizations tougher to lead and that the person who can master it all is the quintessential manager. In the same publication, there were examples of people who had gone from jobs in business to nonprofit institutions thinking it would be "a piece of cake" only to realize how much more difficult the new setting was.

Drucker's insight points to a large part of the misunderstanding about the performance of voluntary organizations. Before we can judge effectiveness, we have to have a clearer picture of what we are looking for. In the case of nonprofit organizations, we need to have a much better grasp of the uniqueness of these organizations, both in the social role they fulfill and in the ways they operate. If we simply apply "bottom-line" efficiency as our standard, we fail to distinguish the special characteristics of dynamic voluntary organizations. Most prior efforts to identify the unique characteristics of nonprofits tended toward quantification, such as the number of board meetings held or the number of clients served, and left out any effort to get at the very spirit and passion that are often the factors that lead to results. Nonprofit organizations can learn a great deal from businesses about good management, bottom-line discipline, people development, evaluation of results, and much more, but these are often not the primary ingredients contributing to effectiveness.

Bit by bit, INDEPENDENT SECTOR, guided by its Leadership and Management Advisory Committee, has endeavored to sharpen our grasp of the differences—and similarities—of business and voluntary operations and how we can help prepare our leaders to fulfill both the unique and the similar attributes of success. For example, in the past several years, we have conducted the Studies in Leadership program, headed by John W. Gardner, which is focused now on the development of neighborhood and community leaders; published the nine-part Nonprofit Management Series, ranging from "The Role of the Board and Board Members" to "Evaluating Results"; encouraged and assisted the establishment of academic centers dealing with nonprofit organizations; and, most recently, published our report "Ethics and the Nation's Voluntary and Philanthropic Community."

With publication of our four-year study, *Profiles of Excellence*, we take our largest step to date to clarify the characteristics of successful voluntary operations. The efforts of E. B. Knauft, Renee

A. Berger, and Sandra T. Gray, along with the dedicated participation of committee members, have produced a remarkably useful combination of evidence, examples, guidelines, and references. Their book is a long-term contribution to otherwise sparse
literature and an immediate help to conscientious board and
staff members. It is a major milestone toward that objective set
by the Organizing Committee twelve years ago: "encouragement of effective leadership and management of philanthropic
and voluntary organizations to maximize their capacity to serve
society."

January 1991   Brian O'Connell
                                        President
                                        INDEPENDENT SECTOR

Preface

Nearly three million nonprofit organizations are at work across the country, engaged in virtually every type of societal activity imaginable. They range dramatically in size and purview — from tiny local groups staffed by a handful of committed volunteers to huge, multipurpose national enterprises with hundreds of employees and yearly budgets in the millions of dollars. The nonprofit sector includes symphony orchestras, foundations, zoos, art museums, and advocacy groups. It embraces neighborhood health clinics, homeless shelters, Girl Scout troops, environmental groups, the United Way, and the American Red Cross. The field, by its very nature, defies neat boundaries.

How then do we measure excellence in a universe so large that even simple generalizations are tricky? What are the appropriate yardsticks of success when financial performance is not the whole story, when the quality of service and dedication of volunteers cannot be measured by numbers? Is the mix of ingredients that makes for excellence in one nonprofit organization transferable to another?

In 1986, INDEPENDENT SECTOR, a national forum of 750 organizations that encourages giving, volunteering, and not-for-profit initiative, undertook to try to identify common attributes that the best nonprofit groups consistently display. If such touchstones could be isolated, we felt, they might help other nonprofit groups build a more solid foundation, improve operations, and amplify their impact.

Can Excellence Be Measured?

At the outset, constructing a definition of "excellence" seemed straightforward, but, in fact, the task turned out to be quite challenging. Scores of books have been written on organizational excellence — including many specifically for the nonprofit world — but the findings offer no clear consensus. One study, measuring twenty-five separate variables of organizational excellence, concluded that the whole process is "an extremely untidy construct" (Campbell, Bownas, Peterson, and Dunnette, 1974). Another reviewed many studies and concluded that the topic is "the most ambiguous in the field of management" (Dalton and others, 1980).

If measuring excellence is an inexact science, the challenge to do so is compounded by the very nature of the nonprofit sector. What, after all, do you measure? Should a nonprofit be judged by its capacity to survive over time, to skillfully adapt to changes and challenges over its life cycle? Or perhaps the best measure is current performance. If so, do we consider the organization's financial condition or the number of people it serves, the size of its membership, the quality of its programs and staff, the extent of volunteer engagement? And what about the spirit of the organization and how it is perceived in its community?

Such questions would seem indispensable to gauging performance in the nonprofit world. But most studies, we found, typically did not ask them; rather, they tried to measure excellence by comparing a nonprofit group with other organizations of the same type or in the same community. In some instances, appraisers used specific criteria to make their judgments; in others, an organization was deemed excellent if two or three independent analysts agreed it was. One study used a panel of judges to systematically evaluate information submitted by nonprofits who entered an annual citywide competition. The organizations considered to be the winners were those judged to be most excellent in their management.

The Scope of This Book

For *Profiles of Excellence,* we sought to go beyond the parameters of most research in the field. We reviewed existing studies of organizational excellence and incorporated their findings where appropriate, but we also endeavored to break new ground through fresh research.

The project consisted of four parts:

1. A thorough examination of more than two hundred existing studies and references on organizational effectiveness
2. A one-day focus group of twenty nonprofit leaders and experienced consultants, convened for a wide-ranging discussion of factors underlying excellence in nonprofits
3. A questionnaire surveying the views of more than nine hundred chief staff officers and board chairs from a national sample of nonprofits
4. In-depth profiles of ten nonprofit groups that a panel of community foundations judged to be especially effective

Our researchers also found five outside studies that were particularly relevant to our topic, and their findings are incorporated here in some detail. Three of the five attempted to isolate the qualities that distinguish excellent nonprofit leadership by comparing successful executives with less successful ones. One study contrasted 14 "effective" advocacy groups with a control group of 100 less effective organizations. The fifth study carefully analyzed 22 nonprofits that had been selected from among 300 candidates as finalists in a major awards competition in Chicago. Our conclusions are thus drawn from an uncommon wealth of data, reflecting the experiences of well over

one thousand diverse nonprofit groups from across the United
States.

The project concentrated primarily on local rather than
national groups and generally did not include religious congre-
ations or nonprofit colleges, universities, and hospitals.

Overview of the Contents

In the pages that follow, we explore four characteristics that
differentiate the great nonprofits from the merely good ones.
The four chapters that make up Part One examine these four
hallmarks of excellence in depth, illustrated with real-world examples. In Part Two, we turn the spotlight on ten excellent nonprofit organizations from across the country. Their individual
stories are profiled in Chapters Five through Fourteen. Part
Three offers specific suggestions to help nonprofit leaders put
each of the four hallmarks of excellence into practice in their
own organizations.

While we hope the information contained herein will be
useful to students of the management sciences by offering a fresh
framework for studying effectiveness in the nonprofit world, our
primary goal is to present a lively discussion of the real-world
challenges confronting nonprofit practitioners who strive every
day to make their organizations the very best they can be.

Acknowledgments

We wish to acknowledge the guidance and support of INDE-
PENDENT SECTOR's Effective Sector Leadership/Manage-
ment Advisory Committee and especially the four chairs of that
committee while the project was underway: Roger Heyns, president, William and Flora Hewlett Foundation; Reynold Levy,
president, AT&T Foundation; Ira Hirschfield, director of philanthropy, Rockefeller Family and Associates; and Fern Portnoy,
president, Portnoy and Associates.

We are also most appreciative of the continuing stimu-
lation and encouragement from Brian O'Connell, president of
INDEPENDENT SECTOR, to adhere to the goal of completing

a volume of broad interest to nonprofit leaders, volunteers, and staff members.

Our special thanks go to Carol Steinbach, contributing editor of the *National Journal,* who helped translate our words into a more readable style. It has been a pleasure to work with her.

The ten case studies in Part Two were possible only with the complete cooperation and assistance of the chief staff officers and the board and staff members of the nonprofit organizations profiled. We thank them for their willingness to be part of this project.

Finally, we gratefully acknowledge the financial support of those organizations that made this project possible: Primerica Foundation, Beatrice Foundation, Exxon Corporation, William and Flora Hewlett Foundation, and AT&T Foundation.

Washington, D.C.   E. B. Knauft
January 1991   Renee A. Berger
                            Sandra T. Gray

The Authors

E. B. Knauft is executive vice president of INDEPENDENT SECTOR, a national coalition of 750 voluntary organizations, corporations, and foundations with the mission of encouraging giving, volunteering, and not-for-profit initiative. He received his A.B. degree in psychology from Oberlin College, his M.S. degree in psychology from Brown University, and his Ph.D. degree from the University of Iowa in industrial and organizational psychology.

Knauft's experience spans both the for-profit and nonprofit worlds. At Aetna Life and Casualty, he served as vice president of personnel and planning and later as vice president of corporate social responsibility and executive director of the Aetna Foundation. In the 1970s, he assisted John Filer in the work of the Commission on Private Philanthropy and Public Needs (the Filer Commission). Knauft has served as chief operating officer of INDEPENDENT SECTOR since 1984. His volunteer activities have included two terms as board chair of the Citizens' Scholarship Foundation of America and board membership in such groups as the Nonprofits' Risk Management & Insurance Institute, Junior Achievement of Central Connecticut, and the Coordinating Council for Foundations in Hartford.

Knauft's publications include *Profiles of Effective Corporate Giving Programs, A Research Agenda for Corporate Philanthropy, Self-Perceptions of Effectiveness: A Survey of Nonprofit Voluntary Organizations, The World of Philanthropy — Looking Into the Eighties,* and *The Filer Commission Revisited.*

Renee A. Berger is president of TEAMWORKS, Inc., a consulting firm formed in 1985 that specializes in survey design and management, program evaluation, strategic planning, and human resources development. Major clients have included Sun Microsystems, the Upjohn Company, Gannett Foundation, Ford Foundation, Pennsylvania Power and Light Company, Wesray Capital Corporation, New York City Partnership, and the White House. Before establishing TEAMWORKS, Berger served as the director of partnerships for the White House Task Force on Private Sector Initiatives and had served as a consultant for numerous organizations in the United States and abroad.

Berger received her B.A. degree in literature and her M.A. degree in planning from the State University of New York at Buffalo. She taught at George Washington University and was a visiting professor at Griffith University in Australia. She frequently guest lectures at universities in the United States and overseas.

Berger is the author of several books and articles. Her major works include *Public-Private Partnership in American Cities: Seven Case Studies* (coedited with R. S. Fosler); *Public-Private Partnership: An Opportunity for Urban Communities* (coauthored with R. S. Fosler); "Private Sector Initiatives in the Reagan Era: New Actors Rework an Old Theme," in *The Reagan Presidency and the Governing of America;* "Corporate Leadership and the Public Weal" (coauthored with M. Sviridoff), in *Executive Talent.*

Sandra T. Gray is a vice president of INDEPENDENT SECTOR and headed the Effective Sector Leadership/Management Program and, more recently, the national "Give Five" campaign. Prior to joining INDEPENDENT SECTOR, she was executive director of the National School Volunteer Program. She was previously an assistant commissioner, U.S. Department of Education; the assistant and policy adviser to the Undersecretary of Education; and HEW fellow and special assistant to the Secretary of Health, Education and Welfare.

As a former university and public education administrator and teacher, Gray worked in five states and served in the administration of two state departments of education. Her current professional interests are issues related to education, the community, and effective leadership.

Gray has served as a community volunteer, working with leaders in government, education, voluntary organizations, foundations, and business to build more effective community partnerships. A recipient of numerous honors and recognitions, Gray was a member of the President's Committee on Educational Partnerships and of a delegation of American women leaders visiting the Soviet Union under sponsorship of the Rockefeller Foundation, and she was designated one of America's top 100 black business and professional women by *Dollars and Sense* magazine.

PROFILES
OF
EXCELLENCE

PART ONE

THE FOUR HALLMARKS
OF EXCELLENCE

———————————◆———————————

Picture a professional orchestra. Its musicians read notes proficiently, play their instruments well, and practice long hours together. But it takes much more to turn them into a world-class symphony orchestra. The same is true for a nonprofit organization. The organization cannot survive without a good board, a competent director, and solid financial controls. Make no mistake on this point: Our hallmarks of excellence are no substitute for sound management practices and effective programs. But it takes more to differentiate a truly great organization from the merely good ones, and the four hallmarks of excellence we describe are the "something extra" that makes all the difference—of a clear and tangible "value added."

The four hallmarks of excellence in nonprofit organizations are:

1. A clearly articulated sense of mission that serves as the focal point of commitment for board and staff and is the guidepost by which the organization judges its success and makes adjustments in course over time.
2. An individual who truly leads the organization and creates a culture that enables and motivates the organization to fulfill its mission.

1

3. An involved and committed volunteer board that relates
    dynamically with the chief staff officer and provides a bridge
    to the larger community.
4. An ongoing capacity to attract sufficient financial and hu-
    man resources.

     Before we examine each hallmark, a caveat is in order.
Effective nonprofits have all four characteristics: a clear mission, strong leaders, a committed board, and stable revenues.
But, as the case studies in Part Two illustrate, even the best
organizations have flaws. Some are reassessing their mission.
A few boards need fine tuning. Not all executive directors share
power effectively with board chairs. And despite the best intentions, fund raising is sometimes shaped by opportunity rather
than strategy. Ideally, an effective organization has all its key
components operating well. In reality, one or two elements may
not be functioning quite as smoothly as the others.

Chapter One

The Primacy of Mission

———————◆———————

The "mission" is an organization's reason for existence. Broad but clear mission statements are written into bylaws, highlighted in brochures, and promoted in fund-raising overtures. The mission is on the tongue of board members and staff—and most important, is reflected in their actions. In other words, effective nonprofit organizations convey a singlemindedness of purpose. Board and staff know exactly what they are offering, and for whom.

The crucial link between mission and performance came up repeatedly in our focus group of nonprofit executives and consultants, and was echoed in our questionnaire results. The chief staff officers and board chairs we surveyed, when asked to list characteristics of an effective organization, answered most often: a clear sense of mission accompanied by goals to carry out that mission. When asked to suggest ways a nonprofit could improve, a majority gave the highest priority to "making mission central." Among the board chairs we surveyed, 82 percent said that a strong mission orientation is the top criterion on which they judge the effectiveness of a chief staff officer (INDEPENDENT SECTOR, 1990b).

The centrality of mission also appears repeatedly in other research. A prime example is the analysis of successful nonprofit executives conducted by the National Assembly of National Voluntary Health and Social Welfare Organizations. "Belief in mission," the study concluded, "is one of the key factors that distinguishes the excellent leader from the run-of-the-mill." Interestingly, a majority of the executives polled in that study said people who knew them best would rate them highest on their ability "to articulate the agency's mission." Or as one successful executive put it: "My responsibility is ensuring we are keeping within our value system and our mission — to make sure that what we are doing is the appropriate thing." A board member interviewed for the study noted that for the successful nonprofit leader, mission "is an avocation as well as a vocation" (National Assembly, 1989, p. 37-38).

Our analysis of data from more than three hundred Chicago-area nonprofits competing in the Beatrice Foundation's awards program offers still more evidence of the tie between mission and excellence. As part of the application process, the groups are asked: "How do you define success and how do you know when you have been successful?" Most of the twenty-two organizations selected as finalists answered "fulfillment of mission." All twenty-two had a clear mission statement. Some measured success in numerical terms. The National Committee for the Prevention of Child Abuse, for example, in 1986 said its mission was to reduce child abuse by 20 percent by 1990. But the lack of quantitative measures did not keep other organizations from placing mission first. The Cambodian Association of Illinois, for instance, said its mission would be fulfilled when "our clients live as comfortable a life in Chicago as possible."

Challenges to the Mission

Effective organizations are not spared challenges to their mission. Quite the contrary. What distinguishes the best groups is their openness to self-assessment, an acceptance of criticism, and a capacity to make the tough decision — whether that means sustaining the original vision or fashioning a new one as the times demand. But there is a fine line between appropriate adjustments in mission and counterproductive diversions. Consider a parallel from the for-profit world. To stay competitive, companies must continually adjust their products and services to fit the demands of the marketplace. But the company that diversifies into a field where it has little experience jeopardizes the financial success of the entire enterprise.

Brian O'Connell sums up the mission challenge this way: "An effective voluntary organization has a capacity to keep the real mission in focus no matter how frenzied things become or how great the pressure to move into new areas. This means that all important decisions are made with the organization's 'reason for being' in the forefront" (1984, p. 4).

Real-world examples may help clarify the issue. Most of the organizations profiled in Part Two have had to revisit their missions at least once over the years. In fact, the particular challenges they confronted are common in the nonprofit world.

Staying the Course. Interlochen in northern Michigan operates a highly succesful music and performing arts summer camp for talented youngsters (see Chapter Ten). But during a rough spot sixteen years ago, the group faced a crucial mission challenge. Interlochen's founder and long-time director had died, prompting the board to hire a new executive. Too late, board members discovered the new director envisioned a different mission: he wanted to transform Interlochen into a summer haven primarily for adults. After a tumultuous period, the board decided to sustain the original mission. It replaced the new director with a former Interlochen camper who had gone on to excel in music education and management. For more than fifteen years, he was the right person for the job.

Shifting Priorities. Harlem's Upward Fund Afterschool began in the 1970s as a basketball academy. Its mission: to encourage athletic excellence as a way of combatting the hopelessness of inner-city poverty (see Chapter Fourteen). From the outset the goal was to use sports as a way to interest Harlem youth in education, but in the early days, education took a back seat. Change came in the course of deliberations over whether to buy a building and convert it into a gym. Upward Fund and its sponsors discovered that several other Harlem basketball programs were already doing an effective job promoting sports. The organization decided to reorient its mission to focus on education, and in 1981 it launched a summer computer day camp. Sports still play an important role, but now youngsters must show academic progress to remain in the program.

Adapting to Changing Times. For nearly half a century, the Atlanta Historical Society (AHS), chartered in 1926, was an exclusive gathering place for Civil War history buffs and the Old South elite. Today, AHS is a dynamic organization serving thousands of present-day Atlantans with exciting exhibits and stimulating programs (see Chapter Five). The transformation did not occur in a vacuum. The organization expanded its funding and physical facilities, made an evolutionary change in board membership and philosophy, and carefully chose a dynamic new executive director. A series of board retreats in 1986 completed the transition. The mission was revised and enlarged to keep pace with the times, with full support and involvement of the board.

Resisting Temptation. The heart of the San Francisco Education Fund (SFEF) is its small grants to reward innovative teachers (see Chapter Twelve). But when the group's reputation began to grow a few years ago, funders came offering money to try new programs. Staff began to lead SFEF into new areas, and there was strong pressure to become more involved in lobbying for systemic changes in the public school system. Board members became enmeshed in heated debate. Some complained bitterly that funders appeared to be dictating priorities, that staffpeople were charging ahead without board approval. The board decided to revisit SFEF's mission and reaffirm board responsibilities. Eventually board members reasserted their stewardship over the staff and relationships with funders became more collaborative.

The temptation to chase the dollars is so pervasive that most nonprofits confront it at one time or another. Effective groups resist the urge to stray too far afield from their mission. As one board member in the National Assembly survey put it, "We have had an opportunity to take on large projects which could mean more staff, bigger dollars and maybe a big initial publicity splash. But our staff executive would not be confused or sidetracked. He doesn't want to build an empire. He focuses on the accomplishments the agency is capable [of] and doesn't waver." (National Assembly, 1989, p. 38)

Ironically, as the experience of the San Francisco Education Fund illustrates, often the most successful nonprofit groups face the staunchest mission challenges. Several finalists in our Beatrice Awards competition, for example, said their most significant challenge was to adhere to their mission and goals in the face of success. The National Committee to Prevent Child Abuse reported that it "guard[s] against distractions from our plan" by persistently monitoring the national staff and the activities of state chapters. The Chicago Association of Neighborhood Development Organizations, another nonprofit with a strong track record, noted that it carefully scrutinizes project proposals based on how each would further the association's mission and long-range goals.

Remaining true to mission can also spell the difference between success and failure when hard times hit. Baxter Community Center in Grand Rapids, Michigan, for instance, has experienced many ups and downs in providing social services to the inner-city poor over two decades (see Chapter Six). The group nearly collapsed several years ago. But its adherence to mission, its unwavering dedication to "providing for basic human needs," enabled Baxter Community Center to weather funding cutbacks and other adversities.

For the nonprofit in search of excellence, mission really matters. There is simply no substitute for a clearly focused statement of purpose. Nonprofit groups that give short shrift to their missions will almost always find the going bumpy. Those that invest the time and effort necessary to formulate a sound mission statement build a platform from which to soar.

Chapter Two

Effective Leadership

The second hallmark of an excellent organization is the presence of a true leader. Much has been written in recent years on the qualities of forceful leaders. The subject defies simple classification, yet the questions persist: What makes leaders stand apart? How does one recognize a leader? What conditions enable leadership to emerge?

Attributes of Leadership

Perhaps the most appropriate starting point is to relate leadership to the first hallmark of excellence — mission. The best leaders, we found, embody their organizational mission. They can clearly articulate the mission and transmit it to others with a sense of excitement, even if the mission was originally developed by a board or a founder long since departed. John Gardner (1990) writes that the first task of leadership is "envisioning goals." Our study confirmed that in the best organizations, the leader and the mission are inseparable.

The best leaders share two other pervasive qualities. They can make the mission come alive in the minds and hearts of others. And they can link an organization's mission to its past and bridge ahead from today's task to the future. As one successful executive in the National Assembly study put it: "Not only must you have a sense of mission, but a sense of vision. Where do you want to go and how are you going to know when you get there? An organization oftentimes takes on the personality and vision of the leader. Where there is no vision, the people perish" (National Assembly, 1989, p. 36). True leaders, says O'Connell, have the "vision to see beyond the horizon, along with sensitivity to really feel human needs, plus an almost contradictory toughness to build an organization capable of translating the vision and sensitivity into change" (1984, p. 4).

The nonprofit organization in search of excellence might now ask: Which leader are you talking about — our volunteer board chair or our executive director? Our focus in this book is primarily on the executive director. In the groups we examined, when true leadership emerged, it was usually the executive director. Most of the organizations we studied had full-time executive directors and staffs, and part-time volunteer boards. (There were exceptions, of course, particularly in new organizations or those in transition.) That is not to say that the board's leadership is unimportant. It is critical; indeed, an effective board is the third hallmark of excellence. When both board and executive directors are strong, an organization's achievement may be magnified many times over.

Our focus group of nonprofit executives singled out leadership as the number-one reason why some groups excel and others do not. From able leadership flow many other elements critical to an organization's success, from garnering resources to attracting volunteers to getting results. The focus group concluded that the best leaders:

- Have clear goals and a vision to look beyond the day's crisis, the quarterly report, the immediate horizon.
- Exhibit a willingness to stand up and be shot at.
- Have the courage to make extremely tough decisions.

- Understand their constituent's motivations and identify intimately with their needs and concerns.
- Exhibit a special presence that enables them to motivate and inspire their constituents, staff, and volunteers beyond the authority conferred by a title.

The sixty outstanding nonprofit leaders interviewed in the National Assembly study (1989) echoed similar themes. In addition to "belief in mission," they said that the key attributes of nonprofit leadership included an entrepreneurial attitude, an action or risk-taking orientation, and vision. The best leaders exhibit a strong belief in self, a willingness to take responsibility for decisions, flexibility in management style, and concern for the people being led and the task to be completed.

The case studies in Part Two present a collective portrait of effective leadership. The directors of these ten organizations are as varied in birth and background as all of America. They are male and female, young and retirement age, white, black, Hispanic, Asian, and American Indian. Some have a good deal of formal education, others are streetwise. A few came up through the ranks of their organization; many were new to it.

Norine Smith, executive director of the Indian Health Board in Minneapolis, is a prime example of entrepreneurial leadership. Her drive, intensity, desire to provide for her constituency, and consuming need to succeed are essential to the survival of the Indian Health Board. She is imaginative, bold, decisive, articulate, passionate, persuasive, convincing — the blueprint of a leader.

An entrepreneurial leader operating in a very different setting is John Ott, executive director of the Atlanta Historical Society. Ott has taken this once elitist society on a vastly broader course, expanding its mission, spurring the professionalization of its staff and board, embracing a larger and more diverse constituency, and diversifying resources. Before Ott came, one board member remarked, "the board was more of a social group. Now it's much more serious. We discuss puzzlements and long-range planning."

A third example of successful leadership is Gene Proctor, executive director of the Baxter Community Center in Grand Rapids. Proctor did not arrive at the center through a systematic search process. He had worked there briefly before leaving for the business world. When the center fell on hard times in the late 1970s, the board asked Proctor to take over. He agreed to come back for ninety days. Ten years later, Proctor is still at the helm and has accomplished a remarkable turnaround.

He did so by concentrating on fundraising and serving as a role model of industriousness with personal commitment to the organization and little tolerance for employees who did not carry their weight. The center relies on funding from the community's predominantly white business leaders. But when Proctor took over, funders were balking. Baxter had lost a major federal services contract and was hemorrhaging financially. Five executive directors had come and gone in only two years. Proctor turned to colleagues with connections in the foundation world. They linked him up with United Way. He forged a new relationship with the Amway Corporation. Eventually, Proctor established a firm funding base. Said one colleague: "His leadership style and integrity inspired confidence among business people. . . . He is humble, isn't macho, doesn't wear Brooks Brothers suits. He knows how to deal with the businessmen at the Peninsula Club, but never forgets his clients." Proctor also did not hesitate to dismiss several employees he inherited from a previous regime, because he quickly recognized they were deadwood to the organization.

The executive directors of the ten organizations profiled in Part Two routinely display the following leadership traits:

Mission-directed. Mission is an all-consuming passion for these ten directors. John Ott erupts with enthusiasm for history. He views the Atlanta Historical Society as his pulpit to convert others. He misses no opportunity to speak to local groups and networks widely to promote the organization to all parts of the community.

Energy and Concentration. Whether comparatively young or nearing retirement, these executive directors have vast reserves of energy and a capacity to channel their vitality. All work longer than normal hours. For Martha Dilts of the Seattle Emergency Housing Services, that means many evenings attending to coalition building, legislative briefings, fund raising, and networking.

Motivator. The ten directors profiled in Part Two inspire their staffs. At Harlem's Upward Fund, everyone agrees Gene Kitt is a remarkable motivator. Comments from staff range from "he really cares about kids" to "Gene is honest" to "he is trying to improve himself all the time." Others note that Kitt "is a good listener," "inspires me with his trust," and "challenges me yet gives me support."

Organizational Self. Rather than seek personal glory, these directors measure success in the achievements of their organizations. As leaders they are tenacious, gritty, and persistent. When the Indian Health Board decided to expand from advocacy to providing primary health care, the group needed money to hire a doctor and dentist. Executive director Norine Smith struck out with forty-nine funders before the Donner Foundation finally said yes. To get needed medical equipment, Smith phoned local hospitals for the names of retired physicians. She then called one doctor after another, explaining the tax deductions they could earn for their donations and offering to come out immediately and pick up the equipment in her truck.

Two-way Communication. A few of the ten directors are very articulate. Others are reluctant to be on stage. One director admitted she is sometimes hard to follow; she is euphemistically described by a board member as "poetic." But all the executives like people and are good at networking. All work very hard at being good listeners. And each seems to reflect the notion that more than word, deed is the measure of great communicators.

Social Antennae. The ten directors are intelligent, but not bookish. Rather, their intelligence is "people sense." Chris Medina of Guadalupe Center in Kansas City overcame resistance from his board to hire Bernardo Ramirez, his deputy. Ramirez had a colorful background, including some brushes with the law. But Medina saw a diamond in the rough — and Ramirez has proved him correct.

Creative Thinking. Most good leaders are creative and innovative. At Harlem's Upward Fund, for instance, Gene Kitt does not simply accept free baseball tickets for his kids from the corporate executives who routinely offer them, he goes one step further. Kitt asks the business leaders to take his youngsters to the games, and then to write letters to the children afterward since his kids so seldom receive any outside recognition.

Leaders Versus Managers

The best nonprofits are both well led and well managed — but not always by the same person. Indeed, a number of leadership studies point out differences between good leaders and good managers.

For Bennis and Nanus (1985), the leader supplies the vision for an organization and mobilizes its emotional and spiritual resources accordingly, while the manager concentrates principally on personnel, technology, and finances. "An excellent manager can see to it that work is done productively and efficiently, on schedule, and with a high level of quality," they write (p. 92). However, they assert, it is the leader's role to help people know pride and satisfaction in their work. "Great leaders often inspire their followers to high levels of achievement by showing them how their work contributes to worthwhile ends" (p. 93).

A survey by the Foundation of the American Society of Association Executives (1989) underscores this view. The study compared "very successful" executives with a group rated as "less successful." The best executives, the study found, were more involved in policy activities, performed a leadership role with staff, concentrated heavily on communications with their boards, and focused on long-range strategic objectives. By contrast, the less successful directors were more involved with administrative matters and tended to focus on short-term activities. The researchers concluded that successful executives do play a strong leadership role, while their less successful counterparts carry out a more conventional management function.

Not that the two roles are necessarily mutually exclusive. John Gardner, for example, lists "managing" as one of the nine tasks of leadership. "Every time I encounter an utterly first-class manager, he turns out to have quite a bit of the leader in him," he writes (1990, p. 4).

Several of the executive directors profiled in the case studies in Part Two are better leaders than managers, more comfortable with the big picture than the intimate details. John Ott of the Atlanta Historical Society, for example, looks to his staff to handle organizational particulars. Gene Proctor, executive director of Baxter Community Center, likewise relies on his deputy to handle internal management. Gladys Thacher, executive director of the San Francisco Education Fund, knows that financial management is not her strong suit, so board oversight in this area is especially thorough, even as Thacher and her staff build their skills.

Leadership and Organizational Culture

One leadership attribute sometimes overlooked is the good leader's ability to create the culture of the organization. A strong leader has the capacity to affect and sometimes change the basic assumptions and beliefs shared by the group.

Every organization has its own unique values. For the nonprofit, these might include a special emphasis on attending to members' concerns, or providing services to clients, or recognizing volunteers. The organizational culture is also reflected in attitudes about the working environment. Do staff believe that creativity and initiative are encouraged, expected, and rewarded? An organization's culture cannot be discerned from its written policies or pronouncements from its executive director or board. But culture largely determines how the staff performs and ultimately, how much an organization achieves.

For E. H. Schein, a senior scholar in the field, the axis between leadership and organizational culture is paramount. "The endless discussion of what leadership is and is not could, perhaps, be simplified if we recognized that the unique and essential function of leadership is the manipulation of culture" (1985, p. 317). Here "manipulation" is used in a positive sense — and it is the true leader's most difficult challenge. A leader must have the vision to create a culture and the ability to articulate and enforce this vision.

Roger Jacobi assumed the presidency of the Interlochen Center for the Arts in a turbulent period and worked quickly to establish a new and different culture. First, Jacobi sent a clear signal of openness to the faculty by making it a condition of his employment that he be free to release to the faculty a recent report critical of Interlochen's management and finances. This report previously had been suppressed at the behest of some board members. Second, he took a strong stand on behalf of a faculty member who had been terminated on the basis of questionable evidence by an interim president. By arranging full compensation for the aggrieved former employee, Jacobi clearly established a climate of fairness in the eyes of the entire faculty.

Finding the Right Leader

"Leaders cannot be thought of apart from the historic context in which they arise, the setting in which they function and the system over which they preside," writes Gardner (1990, p. 1). In other words, finding the right person for the time and place makes the real difference.

In our studies, we found that while good leaders share certain attributes, they are not "generic" so much as individuals performing as leaders in particular situations. The entrepreneurial founder who is so vital to an organization in its startup phase might be inappropriate for a mature group further along in its growth cycle. Likewise, the leader who has successfully headed a slow-growing, stable organization might not be so effective when the group hits a sudden growth spurt or a difficult downturn.

Obviously, nonprofit boards seeking to hire a new executive director must scrutinize candidates carefully—but not merely to see if the person is qualified. The best groups, we found, conscientiously work to ensure a fit between the organization's needs at the time and the perceptions, expectations, and goals of any prospective executive director. As the newly hired director of a major symphony orchestra explained: "I told my wife I was taking the job because I was so impressed with the questions posed by the search committee. This was the first board which had ever asked me to articulate my vision for the future of the orchestra."

Many good organizations have fallen off stride at least once in their history over the question of leadership. After a long-time executive director of the Atlanta Historical Society (AHS) retired, the board replaced him with an "insider" who soon showed he lacked the necessary administrative skills and other abilities required to meet the organization's needs and challenges. When the board decided another change was needed, they vowed not to make the same mistake again. They embarked on a national search, questioned board members of each candidate's present organization, and interviewed finalists in depth about their vision and goals for AHS. The effort paid off—John Ott has proved to be an unusually capable leader.

Nothing tests an organization's mettle like losing a strong executive director. As one board member put it, "To think about his leaving is like thinking about death." Nonprofit organizations are typically leanly staffed, often with no deputy director or analogous position for incubating a successor. Most of the organizations profiled in Part Two chose directors from outside the organization. Only one, Guadalupe Center in Kansas City, specifically groomed a staff member to take over the top leadership job.

Even if they do not groom a successor, good directors help their organizations prepare for future leadership transitions. At Interlochen, for example, executive director Roger Jacobi coached the nominating committee in the attributes needed in a leader who would take the music camp into the next century. Kate Harris at the Northside Center for Child Development made it clear she was not planning to stay indefinitely. In addition to creating a deputy director's position, Harris made sure a leadership team knew the working of her organization.

The Special Role of Ethnicity and Race

Five of the ten organizations singled out for their effectiveness in the case studies are directed by minorities. In each case, the directors' ethnic or racial makeup mirrors the organization's prime constituency. Yet these executives face a special challenge. They must engender the trust of their constituents, even while they cultivate funders and operate within an establishment that tends largely to be white.

Several of the minority directors, like Guadalupe Center's Chris Medina, grew up in the communities where they now work. This is no coincidence. Being from the community boosts credibility. Gene Kitt, who is black, spent his early years in the Harlem neighborhood where his organization, Upward Fund, now concentrates. Norine Smith, director of the Indian Health Board (IHB), grew up on a reservation, not far from IHB's headquarters.

These directors exhibit a special multicultural sensitivity that smooths relationship building with other groups. But it is not always easy. For example, as a result of her effective bridge building with the white community, some Indians derisively labeled Norine Smith an "apple" ("red" only on the outside). But she contends: "We must learn to live in both worlds, keeping the beauty of Indian life, but defeating the ugliness of alcoholism and welfare living."

Gene Proctor of the Baxter Community Center is black. But he is a member of a primarily white, conservative church — and a Republican. Initially, Proctor had difficulty building trust within his own constituency. Today, his track record leaves no doubt about his concern for Grand Rapids's inner-city poor. In fact, Proctor's fellow members at the influential Christian Reform Church, including many of the city's power brokers, paved the way for broader community support.

Some minority directors have had to confront conflicts in cultural values or overcome stereotypes. Lynette Lee, director of the East Bay Asian Local Development Corporation, is a prime example. Lee acknowledges that she is by nature a quiet person. That makes her particularly sensitive to the stereotypical view of Chinese women as deferential to male authority. But Lee's quietness is not timidity — she is a tough and canny politician.

A cultural clash nearly meant collapse for Guadalupe Center several years ago, when the group's board defied the local bishop over a hiring decision. As director Chris Medina explains, Hispanic culture teaches not to challenge elders — especially not in the church. Overcoming a tradition of deference was hard. But the principle of consensus decision making was so important to Guadalupe's board that its members chose to break away from the church.

The leaders of effective nonprofit organizations have developed special personal qualities that set them apart. The best leaders carry with them a guiding vision that they can convey to others with energy and excitement. They understand themselves well, both their special talents and their limitations. They are stubborn enough to stand by their convictions when challenged and yet entrepreneurial enough to admit mistakes or take risks when the need arises.

Chapter Three

A Dynamic Board

The third hallmark of an excellent organization is the presence of an involved and committed volunteer board that relates dynamically with the executive director. The board represents a nonprofit's top level of governance. It is legally responsible for the organization and for hiring, supervising, and when necessary, replacing the executive director.

But in the best nonprofits, the board's role extends far beyond these legal and oversight obligations. And, we found, the impact of an activist and dynamic board can be dramatic. One part of our survey of board chairs and executive directors compared the responses of a sub-sample drawn from organizations known for their excellence with the total national sample. The respondents from the excellent organizations gave a rating to the importance of the board as a key factor in overall organizational effectiveness twice as high (80 percent) as did the total sample of respondents.

Characteristics of an Effective Board

In the best nonprofits, the board and executive director forge a special working relationship, grounded in mutual trust and responsibility, two-way communications, and power sharing. The board is fully informed about all the workings of the organization, but it remains focused on general policy and long-range goals. In all but very small or emerging groups, the responsibility for day-to-day management is delegated to the executive director.

The dynamic board also pays close attention to the character and diversity of its membership. It regularly seeks out "new blood," not only as a source of new ideas, but to renew itself and adapt to changing circumstances in ways that help the organization achieve its mission.

As we shall see in the next chapter, the good board is also actively involved in fund raising. Board members decide when to initiate fund raising and membership campaigns. They identify and call on potential contributors. When appropriate, they make personal financial contributions.

Finally, in the best organizations, the board chair is fully dedicated to the organization's mission and prepared to give sufficient time and attention to the task. The post is one of high responsibility.

A Special Working Relationship

In their study of fifty nonprofits in Kansas City, researchers Herman and Heimovics (1987) uncovered a number of vital building blocks of an effective partnership between a nonprofit's board and its executive director. Interestingly, they discovered that in both very effective groups and less effective ones, executive directors and boards reported being in frequent contact. But in the best groups, they found, the relationship reflects much more. The board is actively involved in broad policy matters. Lines of responsibility between the director and board are clearly drawn. Mutual trust is high and nurturing it is a priority. The most effective executive directors willingly provide critical information to their boards, not to engage board members in daily management operations but to help them feel comfortable and confident about the status of affairs in the organization.

Other studies underscore these points. The National Assembly (1989), for example, found that the best executive directors display a flexible relationship with their boards and operate in a "supporting and guiding" manner. Another study, by the Foundation of the American Society of Association Executives (1989), found that the most successful executives are far more likely to communicate regularly and in person with their boards. They also strive to differentiate responsibilities — the board's to make policy, the executive director's to execute it.

How do such qualities translate in human terms? A board chair in the National Assembly study (1989, p. 67) described his group's executive director in these words: "Jim has a lot of respect with board members. He has recruited good people for the board. They are an active and listening board. Some boards I've known are just 'rubber stamps' or 'railway stations.' But Jim has handled this board well, from the standpoint of getting every board member involved in committees, fundraising and other ventures."

Jim, in turn, assesses his board this way: "I feel very strongly that staff is in a partnership role with the board; that one is not subservient to the other, that we work with a team approach on things. . . . I see my role definitely as the one who keeps hitting them with new ideas. But at the same time, there is an atmosphere of comfortable mutual trust because the board knows my interest is what is best for the agency. There is trust on their part that I am not going to do things that they are unaware of, that I am going to work within the parameters we have all agreed on."

Among the groups spotlighted in our case studies, boards range from highly sophisticated to relatively uninvolved. The board of the Seattle Emergency Housing Service (SEHS) is first rate. A former board president insists there are "no tricks, no magic" — just people willing to work hard to achieve the mission. Meetings are monthly; committee work requires extra time. Special events add to a board member's busy agenda but are well attended nonetheless. Retreats and fund raisers, for instance, get close to 100 percent participation.

SEHS's process for bringing on new board members is especially noteworthy. Candidates first meet with current board members to learn about the SEHS mission, its structure, and what is expected of them. They next meet with the executive director and other staff, then attend a board meeting before making a decision to join. The process, says one board member, is meant to convey that "we're not elitist, we all want to participate, and we battle over ideas and keep that separate from the individual."

Retreats

Many organizations use board retreats to reexamine their mission, make long-range plans, create rapport among board members, and strengthen relations between the board and executive director. Most groups report that retreats do improve communications and enhance the sense of mutual goals and camaraderie. Some groups wait until a crisis hits to schedule a retreat; others hold them at least once a year. The Seattle Emergency Housing Service has two annual retreats, one for fund raising and another for strategic planning. Some organizations hire professional facilitators to help with specific tasks or to mediate particularly difficult issues. Typically, the executive director is the only staff member present at the board retreat.

For the Atlanta Historical Society, board retreats provided the right forum several years ago for revamping and revitalizing the mission. Critical decisions faced the board. Some members wanted AHS to remain a "members only" organization; others favored opening it up to Atlanta's general public. An experienced consultant guided the process. Eventually, the board adopted the more expansive vision for the society.

Adapting to Change

A recurrent theme in the profiles of excellent organizations is their capacity to change as the times demand. That applies as well to boards of directors. The best groups accompany changes in their mission with appropriate adjustments in the size and composition of their boards. Sometimes there is a need to bring more diversity to the board as a young organization grows and expands. Sometimes, the board seeks out members with special skills, especially in areas such as fund raising. In other cases, unwieldy boards must be pared.

The San Francisco Education Fund, for example, intentionally began with a small board for its first year to build a team. The strategy worked. At the Atlanta Historical Soceity, on the other hand, board committees were proliferating; at one point, there were more than twenty. The Indian Health Board, too, suffered from being too ingrown and narrowly focused. In both cases, boards had to be streamlined.

A board can become too large because of a reluctance to drop nonparticipating members. Removing board members is never uncomplicated. Guadalupe Center addressed the problem by devising a strict attendance policy. The Atlanta Historical Society created a special board category for veteran members who could no longer fulfill their time obligations.

When the East Bay Asian Local Development Corporation incorporated in 1975, its ten-member board consisted primarily of Chinese-American student activists, intent on converting a vacant building in Oakland's Chinatown neighborhood into a convalescent facility. The board had time and energy, but no contacts and no real leadership. With funding from a local community foundation, the board held a retreat. Members came to terms with the need to bring aboard a more experienced chair. Business professionals were added and board membership diversified. The reconstituted board, more powerful and savvy, won new operating support grants from public and private sources and acquired the largest parcel of commercial real estate in Chinatown.

Another kind of evolution occurs when founding board members depart. Sometimes the transition brings conflict. The six members of the San Francisco Education Fund's (SFEF) founding board, for example, were all prominent in the community. "Starting small helped to establish strong bonds, as everyone had to carry responsibility and work as a team," one member recounted. SFEF grew quickly and won several major grants awards. Gradually, board membership expanded. In 1985, after serving two consecutive three-year terms, most of the founders departed. "You must get off and let new people in," one member noted. "A board must refresh itself." But the transition was hardly problem free. The staff knew the original board so well that SFEF operated "like one big family." The executive director had to devote more time to briefing the less seasoned board. And the board had to grapple with conflicts over SFEF's mission before the transition could be completed.

Some nonprofits tend to treat their boards like junior partners, whose contributions are important but not paramount. For the nonprofit in search of excellence, such a relationship is not enough. The best nonprofit boards not only ensure sound management of their organizations, but energetically provide direction and initiative. They are full working partners in the truest sense.

Chapter Four

Strong
Development Programs

———————◆———————

The final hallmark of an excellent organization is the capacity to attract and sustain sufficient financial resources. That nonprofit groups face unrelenting pressure to raise funds is axiomatic. Most devote a great deal of time and energy to the pursuit, using a variety of different and often highly imaginative approaches. The universe of funders is eclectic and diverse. Many sources — from foundations to corporations to individuals to governments — typically fall on a nonprofit's list of "possibles." Rarely, however, is one funding source adequate to cover a group's ongoing expenses.

Our focus group of nonprofit executives and consultants listed "the ability to attract resources" as one of the three most crucial factors determining the success of a nonprofit, on par with "leadership" and "clarity of mission." And by a wide margin, the chief staff officers we surveyed considered fund raising the most pressing challenge facing their organizations in the coming three to five years. Interestingly, these executives reported that building fund-raising skills was the area where they perceived the greatest need for personal development. The National Assembly study echoed a similar theme (1989, p. 49). As one executive in that survey put it: "For our agency, fund raising is absolutely critical. A good 50 percent [of our effort] is securing major gifts. All nonprofit CEOs need to realize that [fund raising] is their major role. It can't be delegated to a development person or someone else."

Despite its importance, however, resource development often tends to be opportunistic rather than strategic. Many organizations consider the very notion of outlining a comprehensive fund-raising strategy a luxury.

Sharing Responsibility Enhances Returns

Many nonprofit groups, we discovered, delegate prime responsibility for raising resources to the executive director. The extent of board involvement varies dramatically. At the Indian Health Board in Minneapolis, for instance, virtually all fund-raising tasks fall to the executive director, Norine Smith. Her consumer-oriented board is largely without connections. Smith has borne her role admirably. But the strategy of relying solely on her is risky; success revolves largely around Smith and people she has come to know. The wiser course would be to institutionalize fund-raising capacity in the organization itself.

Nonprofit organizations tend to have little trouble recruiting board members for their special expertise in such areas as public relations, social services, or management—but not fund raising. One common problem is the failure to inform board members beforehand that they are expected to help raise money. Another is inappropriate recruiting of people who may be interested in fund raising but are ill prepared to do so.

Two groups among the ten profiled in Part Two stand out for their fund-raising practices. In both organizations, boards are intimately involved in every stage of the process. The board members of one group are prominent in the community and experienced fund raisers. The other board is more grassroots, but it has been equally successful and creative in securing resources.

Because its mission is to dispense grants, the San Francisco Education Fund (SFEF) was designed from the outset to be a fund-raising organization. The founders knew how to raise money and carefully recruited other board members with similar skills. Fund raising has always been a joint responsibility of board and staff, although the division of tasks has not always been clear. Candid dialogue between SFEF's board and executive director clarified expectations. By mid-1989, the organization had raised a $3.3 million endowment. A yearly luncheon to celebrate public schools nets over $100,000.

The board of the Seattle Emergency Housing Service (SEHS), on the other hand, is noteworthy for its humble origins. Each board recruit is asked to seek $25 contributions from five friends. The request may not be large, but it does help SEHS assess the commitment of potential board members. Among the group's novel fund-raising activities is an annual phonathon, where current and former board members command the phones for two nights to raise needed capital. To minimize fund raisers' anxiety, each member receives a special script, outlining SEHS's mission and detailing how many nights of shelter a donor's gift will buy. As important as the money raised, the phonathon is a baptism for the board.

The Local Philanthropic Culture

In the course of our interviews, nonprofit staff and board members frequently cited their community philanthropic culture as a key factor in fund-raising success. In San Francisco, for example, the affluent population is renowned for its generosity with time and money. A similar culture prevails in Minneapolis. Says Norine Smith of the Indian Health Board: "It's better here. Funders are wonderful and you can talk to them. Most everyone else is just plain sensible and wants to help."

In Grand Rapids, Michigan, the local culture is shaped by the Christian Reform Church, which counts among its members the chief executive officer of Amway Corporation and many senior executives from other area companies. For nonprofit organizations such as Baxter Community Center, being tied in to the church from the beginning through prominent active board members has helped raise funds from the business community and local philanthropies.

Sources of Support

Rare indeed is the nonprofit that raises all its money from a single funding source. None of the ten exceptional groups spotlighted in our case studies did so. Each raised money to cover operating and program needs from a range of funders.

Securing initial operating support and then sustaining it have been the most serious financial hurdles. Most nonprofits, in fact, confront this same challenge. A prime reason is that funders, particularly in the private sector, show a strong bias to fund programs, not operations. The funder that provides multiyear operating support is extremely rare. As a result, nonprofit groups tend to follow a typical funding pattern. They struggle along initially on volunteers' "sweat equity," until they win support for a particular program. The program funds are usually sufficient to cover a staff position and possibly some office essentials.

Five of the ten profiled organizations have successfully tapped their local United Way for support. These funds typically help defray operating expenses, regardless of whether the dollars are designated as operating or program support. Many of the groups have also benefitted from other types of United Way assistance, ranging from funds to improve board operations to evaluation and training. The five groups that do not receive United Way funds are probably ineligible because their missions do not coincide with United Way priorities.

Guadalupe Center in Kansas City has been a United Way agency virtually since its founding. Executive director Chris Medina explains that without this uninterrupted assistance, the organization would probably have shut down. Seattle Emergency Housing Service, too, clearly owes its stability in part to its special relationship with the local United Way. At the Northside Center for Child Development in Harlem, the proportion of United Way funding is relatively small. But the organization did receive crucial support to undertake a board assessment that proved to be a watershed. United Way also recommended strategic funding and improved evaluation for the Indian Health Board in Minneapolis. As a result, board members began taking courses to better understand and fulfill their governing responsibilities.

Being Candid with Funders

Nonprofit groups are quite naturally reluctant to tell funders about things that are not going well. As one director told us: "It's a double-edged sword. I really want to be candid, but not at the risk of punishing the organization." Sometimes, however, funders can help.

When the East Bay Asian Local Development Corporation (EBALDC) encountered board problems, it confided in the San Francisco Foundation. The philanthropy, itself undergoing rapid growth and change, was sympathetic to providing grants to strengthen the organizational skills of its grantees. The foundation paid for an EBALDC retreat, which succeeded in helping the nonprofit move beyond a thorny impasse.

Money is a critical fuel needed to propel a nonprofit organization. But too many groups permit the unending quest for vital resources to blur their true sense of purpose. The nonprofit in search of excellence knows only too well the importance of financial stability. But the best groups also understand that successful fund raising is achieved not through happenstance but through a concerted and coordinated strategy.

PART TWO

EXCELLENCE IN ACTION: CASE STUDIES OF OUTSTANDING NONPROFIT ORGANIZATIONS

It all sounds so clear on paper. Surveys, research studies, and the literature on leadership all help us understand what makes organizations effective. The same four hallmarks of excellence — clear mission, strong leadership, dynamic board, and adequate resources — appear repeatedly in the best groups. But while identifying the building blocks of excellence is straightforward, putting them into practice can seem daunting. For this, there is no substitute for examples from the real world.

We now turn to case studies of ten excellent nonprofits to see how the pieces fit together in functioning organizations. These ten organizations are quite different from one another, and in that respect reflect the wide diversity of the nonprofit world. Each has many strengths and some areas where improvement is needed; none is perfect. But keep in mind that each organization has a history long enough to take it through several evolutionary stages. All achieved excellence over a period of years, partly through trial and error, by learning from their mistakes. Their stories are offered here in the hope that other nonprofits can benefit from their accumulated experiences.

The ten organizations were carefully selected. We started by asking twenty community foundations around the country to nominate nonprofit voluntary organizations in their city or

31

region that they considered particularly effective. They were asked to use a detailed form to evaluate the organizations on a list of criteria, with the important caveat that no organization is likely to be equally strong in all areas of performance.

A total of fifty nominations were received from ten community foundations. A ten-member judging committee — consisting of chief executives of national nonprofits, academic researchers in the nonprofit field, experienced consultants, and senior members of the INDEPENDENT SECTOR staff — then reviewed the nominations, focusing on diversity of type, size, geographical location, and racial characteristics, as well as evidence that candidates were especially effective in their field of activity. Ten organizations were selected for in-depth case studies, all but one of them local in nature, with local boards. The case studies were written by Renee Berger after on-site visits, interviews with the chief staff officer, board chair, and other staff and board members, and a review of available documents.

Chapter Five

Atlanta Historical Society: Adapting to Changing Times

———————◆———————

Chartered in 1926, the Atlanta Historical Society (AHS) used to be the quintessential "old boys" gathering spot, where Civil War battles were re-fought ad nauseum. Very clubby, white, and genteel — this was where history started and ended for Atlanta's elite.

But no more. Today at this historical society, visitors young and old queue up to see blockbuster exhibits. Here you will find archives of the state's first black legislator and an exhibit about segregation. You can hear the latest commentary on presidential politics by *Washington Post* reported David Broder and native Atlantan Judy Woodruff, anchorwoman for *MacNeil-Lehrer News Hour,* or get an insider's view of writing historical novels from writers Alex Haley and John Jakes.

"We'll do anything to help the image of this organization," says John Ott, the society's flamboyant executive director. Ott might be seen riding around town in a red convertible one day, then bedecked in an antebellum costume the next. The point, he explains, is "to say we're fun, we're not aloof, we're part of the community."

A generation ago, Atlanta was still a sleepy southern city. By the 1980s, it had become the transportation and financial services hub for the new South. "Hot"-lanta became the slogan to characterize its feverish entrepreneurial pace.

As change overtook Atlanta, the Atlanta Historical Society joined in its moveable feast of new people and fresh ideas. But change was not easy. It required a major organizational overhaul — enlarging AHS's funding base and physical facilities, revamping its operations, bringing aboard aggressive new leadership, and ultimately refashioning the society's mission. There were false steps along the way and plenty of internal debates. But AHS emerged from the process a dynamic and spirited organization, very much attuned to the modern era and yet still true to it mission and roots.

The Atlanta Historical Society is not perfect. Sometimes too little attention is paid to organizational details. But AHS embodies the four hallmarks of an exemplary organization. It is clear and focused today about its mission. Its leadership is entrepreneurial and bold, capable of generating excitement and infusing energy in a subject — history — that many find dull. Its board has been restructured, its operations streamlined. And it has an enviable resource base, including valuable properties and a sizable endowment, operating in a supportive philanthropic community with a board experienced in fund raising.

Adapting to Changing Times

How did AHS change from an elitist private club to a major public institution?

The transformation took almost two decades. A series of watershed board retreats in 1986 consummated the transition, but the change actually began in 1965, when the society received a $7 million endowment from its founder, Walter McElreath. AHS used the new funds to begin acquiring historic properties. In 1966, it bought Swan House, the premier work of Atlanta's renowned classical architect, Philip Trammell Shutze, a treasure chest of collector's items and historic memorabilia. Soon after, AHS purchased the Tullie Smith House, another historic property.

The inward-looking organization was now clearly set on another path. But even as AHS was evolving into a bigger institution, it remained an exclusive club, frozen in time, almost untouched by the economic growth and social changes sweeping Atlanta. Gradually, board members began to raise significant questions. Would AHS continue to be an elite enclave, devoted to microscopically analyzing the Civil War and collecting and preserving documents? Or would it use its new wealth and opportunity to broaden its mission and embrace the general public?

By 1980, the society had acquired several more buildings and had built new administrative offices, a library, and additional archive space. But despite the many outward changes, AHS's inner workings remained essentially unchanged. Even the new administrative building was planned around sustaining the society's "members only" policy. And the board remained exclusively white male, save for one woman, Louise Allen, wife of former Atlanta mayor Ivan Allen, Jr., who in 1966 became AHS's first female trustee.

The rapid growth had brought the society to a dramatic crossroads. Board members began demanding a more professional staff. The longstanding debate over the AHS mission heated up. Still, AHS had no long-range plan. Finally the missing piece that would solidify the society's transformation arrived — in the person of John Ott.

Entrepreneurial Leadership

When William Pressly retired as executive director in 1978, the board sought another "insider" to run the society, eventually selecting a local scholar with minimal administrative experience. The new director's tenure was brief. In 1981, for the first time since its founding, the board ventured beyond its own small circle to find an administrator. They hired a professional administrator from the midwest. By mid-1982 they realized they had made a mistake. "We hired someone without checking him out as carefully as we should have," says board member Louise Allen. "The chemistry didn't work out."

Again, the board reassembled, this time determined not to repeat their errors. Names were informally collected by a board search committee. Ott emerged as the leading candidate. "We decided to go look at the rabbit in the briar patch," Allen explains. The committee members visited Ott on his own turf. They thoroughly checked his references. They asked his board about his character and communications skills. And they invited Ott to give a presentation to the AHS board.

When Ott was hired in 1983, he knew nothing about the history of Atlanta. In fact, Ott was born in Canada and reared in the North. But he had been a professional museum administrator and had overseen historic properties. And his enthusiasm was infectious.

The new director immediately launched the society on a much broader course, revisiting and expanding its mission, spurring the professionalization of its staff and board, embracing a larger constituency, and diversifying its resources. Before Ott came, Allen notes, "the board was more of a social group. Now it's much more serious. We discuss puzzlements and long-range planning."

Ott, forty-five, symbolizes the new Atlanta. His speech is dotted with statistics on its economic and cultural virtues. "Atlanta is open, permeable, fast-paced—not Brahmin," he says. Ott is an extrovert who really likes people and loves the Atlanta Historical Society. A visitor immediately senses his fervor for history, his conviction to present both its pleasant and unpleasant sides, and his desire to champion history to all Atlantans.

"Part of John's effectiveness is his outreach to assist other organizations," notes one board member. The impact, AHS trustees say, is to bring the society's message to more audiences. A member of many civic and professional organizations and a good public speaker, Ott is an inveterate meeting goer. He is very canny about building a network and using it to find prospective employees, catch up on the local gossip, and make a few more converts.

John Ott is a study in leadership skills. He is, as one AHS staff member put it, "the shirt-sleeves type who doesn't hide in his office." Other staffers characterize Ott as a good listener, ethical, even-tempered, and accessible. He is described as having high energy, excellent communication skills, and a good sense of humor.

Board members especially note Ott's effervescence. He does not get defensive and is always able to find the bright side, board members say. For some, Ott's style is too freewheeling, and periodically he needs to be reigned in. Known for speaking his mind, and even for taking what might be considered political positions (on such issues as preservation versus development, for example), he has been gently warned by a few trustees to tell them beforehand what he is going to say in public.

But Ott, who seems to have more of the soul of an artist than of an administrator, takes the criticism in stride. He strongly believes politics can be an appropriate arena for a historical society. The problem, he says, is not his positions but the twinge of uncertainty among board members that goes with greater public visibility. Interpreting criticism in an organizational context, rather than taking it personally, helps Ott retain the board's strong support.

Board Retreats Clarify New Role, New Structure

Former AHS administrator William Pressly, who had become a trustee, suggested a board retreat for the express purpose of revisiting the society's mission. Ott jumped on the idea. The board liked it too, in part because the suggestion had come from one of its own. Through its extensive network of contacts, AHS was able to enlist the *pro bono* services of one of America's preeminent management consulting firms, McKinsey and Company. No reports were written, and the process was relatively loose — some interviews with staff and two full board retreats. Attendance was excellent and Ott was the only staff member present.

The retreats zeroed in on AHS's vision. Issues ranged from limiting the audiences and retaining a "members only" policy to embracing all the publics that make up the metropolitan Atlanta area. From the outset, it was clear that the bigger picture needed to be resolved before implementation strategies could be tackled — even though the process required a high tolerance for ambiguity.

AHS's trustee handbook (a relatively recent document) describes the outcome: "The Board adopted a vision of presenting the entire story of Atlanta's history in a variety of exciting ways to an increased number of visitors." The handbook goes on: "The target audience is the appreciative, general-interest visitor." This was certainly a far cry from the earlier AHS, with its predominant focus on scholars.

Some in the old guard were not sold on this new broader community outreach. But they recognized that AHS was, as Allen astutely observed, "becoming a public company." Today, the visitor queue might include school children about to be squired through a museum tour on segregation, or a cadre of Japanese business executives clutching glossy AHS brochures (conveniently translated into Japanese).

The retreat series was a watershed for AHS. According to one board member, "We knew we were focusing on minutiae. The retreat gave us an honorable way of disposing of the unproductive practices and set the stage for us to use more effective ones."

Along with vision clarification, the retreat also prompted a massive review of board practices and structure. The board had been creating new committees at a rate that could rival rabbits reproducing; at one point there were twenty-three. Sitting through committee reports at the monthly trustees' meetings had become an endurance contest. The twenty-three committees were collapsed into four groups: executive, oversight, policy, and advisory.

The executive committee was empowered to make some decisions without the approval of the full board, such as hiring and supervising the executive director, allocating the budget, and monitoring committees. The oversight committees (finance, investment, and long-range planning) were designed to zero in on resources. The policy committees (library/archives, marketing/public affairs, museums, and education) were made responsible for guiding programs and ensuring that AHS stay on course. Advisory committees were asked to cover a wide range of areas: physical grounds, collections, publications, membership.

This massive restructuring meant big changes. One dilemma, familiar to many a board, was how to handle longstanding board members who did not want to commit the time and energy now expected of them. The society wanted to sustain a connection with these members, but it also needed to slenderize the board. As a solution, AHS devised an "emeritus member" classification. And as inactive or superfluous board committees were whittled away, "advisory committees" were created to provide a means of continuing involvement.

The board was not the only part of AHS to receive attention; the consultants also looked at the staffing. They recommended creating a new position: assistant to the executive director. Ott, they said, was spread much too thin.

Ott readily acknowledges detail is not his strong suit. He is, in his own words, the "360-degree type who's more adept at shaping the big picture than writing out a management plan." The board is holding his feet to the fire, however. It has asked to see just such a management plan. Each senior manager has been asked to write one; Ott will consolidate the materials into a cohesive whole.

Resource Development

AHS's yearly budget exceeds $2 million. Few nonprofit organizations have had the good fortune to receive so considerable a gift as the McElreath bequest. Investment income from the bequest provides 40 percent or more of AHS annual revenues. But though this is certainly a sizable cushion, no one is resting yet. The remainder of the society's resource base is diverse: fundraising events (12 percent); fees for services (12 percent); membership dues (8 percent); and corporate and foundation grants (18 percent); government funds contribute the smallest portion of overall revenues—7 percent. An important boost for AHS is its longstanding relationship with the Robert W. Woodruff Foundation. The foundation funds capital activities and routinely assists universities and others in Atlanta to acquire and build properties.

Special events are an important element: AHS sits on

some of the most beautiful property in the South, a thirty-two-acre wooded estate in Buckhead, one of the city's most exclusive neighborhoods. The magnificent, historic Swan House is the gathering spot for AHS's annual ball. The event is planned entirely by volunteers, and is always a highlight of the social season. More than five hundred attend, and in 1988, the ball generated more than $300,000.

Swan House, the Buckhead setting, and AHS's connections to Atlanta's affluent community give the society considerable leverage in the business of fund raising. But AHS has elected not to grow complacent about its assets. Organizing the ball, for example, is extremely demanding. Yet each year more volunteers offer to help. Ott is extremely attentive to giving them recognition. According to one observer, "with his southern manners, you'd never know he's a Yankee."

Membership is another area that Ott has emphasized since his arrival. In the past five years, it has more than doubled. Getting new members, however, is not the only way to measure success. Since 1983, the number of AHS members who renew their memberships has jumped from below 50 percent to over 80 percent. The graduated membership fee structure ranges from $15 for students up to $5,000 for some corporate contributors. In the old days — just five years ago — membership development was not a priority. "The system wasn't designed to really respond to members' needs, and the technology wasn't there to run it in a timely manner," says Cynthia Freeman, membership director. Today the old manual system has been computerized. "We make sure the members feel like they belong [and] own a piece of something special," Freeman explains. "Before when someone had a question or a complaint, it went unanswered or festered. Now members are treated individually and with respect for their concerns and ideas."

Looking to the Twenty-First Century

Today, AHS is very much a "public company." Its physical presence has expanded, now reaching from exclusive Buckhead to its new downtown information center. Membership rolls are swelling, attendance is rising, and the collections are getting fatter. More special programs are being introduced. But Ott and his board are not through.

Growth has pushed AHS's facilities to their limits. In late 1988, the board approved plans to construct another building on the Buckhead grounds. To get the ball rolling, AHS hired a professional fund-raising firm. As 1989 drew to a close, the society embarked on the early tasks of learning the steps involved in that process.

A historical society should be a living microcosm of its community. AHS is. Look in one end of the telescope and you see the Atlanta Historical Society. Invert it and you see the broader community.

Chapter Six

Baxter Community Center:
Getting an Agency
Back on Its Feet

———————◆———————

The year is 1978, and the ninety-year-old school building that houses the Baxter Community Center in Grand Rapids, Michigan, is in trouble. The ceiling is filled with asbestos fibers; on hot days, the windows ache with reluctance when you try to push them open, while on cold days, they provide little protection from the frigid blasts of western Michigan winters. The boiler breaks and it's nearly the last straw. Baxter already owes more than $30,000 in unpaid taxes, payroll obligations, and delinquent payments due the building's owner. A new boiler will cost another $7,000. Some think the center should shut down. But that would mean eliminating vital recreation and day-care services for hundreds of poor people in Grand Rapids's inner city.

A dozen years later, the Baxter Community Center is thriving. In January 1990, workers put the finishing touches on a massive renovation of Baxter's building. A capital campaign to transform the group's quarters, undertaken in 1988, raised $1 million in a few short weeks, thanks to support from the Grand Rapids business community. The successful campaign and the speedy completion of the renovation have announced to all that Baxter Community Center, once poorly managed and fiscally irresponsible, has turned the corner.

Many factors helped Baxter Community Center get back on its feet, but its unswerving dedication to mission was paramount. The commitment, rooted in the philosophies of the Christian Reformed Church, which helped found the center and has long helped to maintain it, approaches the evangelical.

Baxter's executive director, Eugene Proctor, is a dynamic leader. He moves easily between the largely black, inner-city world that the center serves and the predominantly white business community that supports the organization. Not long ago, some worried that the center's reliance on Proctor's inspirational leadership left the group organizationally weak. For too long, the board had been only observers. But structural changes have been coming, gradually, with prodding from funders and the spirited leadership of a board member who launched a strategic planning process. By 1990, the board had become a solid, working entity.

The Rise, the Fall, and the Rebirth

The Grand Rapids telephone directory abounds with names like Holland and Zeeland, signaling that this part of Michigan was founded by the Dutch. The hardworking and enterprising Dutch built a community known for its pleasant quality of life. It is also a profoundly religious community, dominated by the fundamentalist and politically conservative. Sunday services admonish parishioners to be industrious and to share their bounty with the less fortunate. In Grand Rapids, most of the churches are Christian Reformed; their membership is almost exclusively white.

In the 1960s, Grand Rapids was not spared the racial unrest that hit larger cities. That experience prompted church elders to begin a social services program in the inner city. This seed grew into Baxter Community Center, incorporated in 1967. Housed initially in a storefront, the center bought its school building from the church at concessionary rates.

For its first ten years, the center grew rapidly. Its modest church support was supplemented with huge grants and contracts from the federal government. This was no accident. Grand Rapids's powerful Congressman, Gerald Ford, interceded on Baxter's behalf. Funds from the Comprehensive Employment Training Act flowed in. By the mid-1970s, Baxter was receiving almost half a million dollars annually, and its staff had grown to more than thirty.

But by 1978, the federal money had stopped coming. Bills were mounting. The building was deteriorating. Baxter had had five executive directors in less than two years. The board, composed mainly of church elders, asked Gene Proctor to take over. An active member of the Christian Reformed Church, Proctor, who is black and a Republican, had briefly served as the center's assistant director in 1971, before leaving for work in the auto industry.

Grand Rapids's black community was initially somewhat dubious. Though Proctor had lived in Grand Rapids for decades and had served in numerous local organizations, including a stint as president of the local chapter of the National Association for the Advancement of Colored People, his political and church involvements were viewed as odd. But in time, Proctor's curious hybrid of affiliations proved to be crucial in helping the center gain access to the city's powerful corporate community.

At first, Proctor agreed to take the job for ninety days. His friends thought he was crazy. Proctor turned to colleagues from a church camp who were affiliated with the local Steelcase Foundation; they put Proctor in touch with United Way of Kent County. Meanwhile, he also contacted Paul Collins, a respected black artist with strong connections in the white community. Proctor had already appealed to Amway, the giant consumer corporation headquartered outside Grand Rapids, but had made no headway. Collins was a friend of two Amway executives. Proctor got his audience.

"I believed in Paul and believed in Gene," recalls Casey Wondergem, Amway's director of public affairs. Wondergem remembers that he thought "it would be a tragedy to let Baxter

be ignored." But, he continues, "Amway did not want to be part
of a salvage operation. After the boiler it would be the windows,
or something else." So Wondergem offered to create a Business
Advisory Committee to familiarize local business executives with
the center and provide assistance when appropriate. But first,
he wanted a commitment from Proctor to stay at least three
years. Proctor agreed. Wondergem's panel formed.

Baxter Community Center already had a board. What
would be the role of the new advisory committee? Establishing
a satellite panel to assist with emergency fund raising could be
taken as a sign that the center's board was too weak. "We didn't
want publicity," says Wondergem. "Keeping a low profile helped
cement our relationship." Amway agreed to come through with
$10,000. United Way followed suit. The center paid off its bills
and repaired the boiler. Baxter was back in business.

A Capital Campaign

Over the years, the Business Advisory Committee's membership has more than doubled (business executives are routinely
invited to the center for lunch), but the panel has remained carefully focused. Each year it raises $25,000 to $30,000 to offset
what would otherwise be an operating deficit at the center. That
had been the extent of the relationship until 1988, when Proctor proposed a massive capital campaign to renovate the center's
26,000-square-foot building.

At the time, the structure violated most of the city's building codes. The windows stuck, the heating system did not work,
there was no air conditioning, toilets were in short supply and
often inoperable, and there were mounting concerns over safety.
Only Baxter's contacts at City Hall, Proctor says, kept it from
being cited. Staff morale was eroding.

A local developer approached Proctor, offering to pay an
architect to draw up plans for the building's renovation. The
estimated cost of the whole project was $500,000. Daunted but
not deterred, Proctor worked his network. He received pledges
of $250,000 from the Steelcase Foundation and the Grand Rap-
ids Community Foundation. He next turned to the Business

Advisory Committee. Wondergem, who had continued to lead the panel, asked a contractor he knew to look at the renovation plans. Cost figures were revised upward, to almost $1 million.

Wondergem's panel committed to raising the funds, but there was a hitch. The United Way of Kent County wanted grantees to have its blessing before launching a capital campaign. Given United Way's powerful connections in Grand Rapids's tightly interwoven business community, it was imperative that Baxter receive consent, but United Way was reluctant to support Baxter's request. United Way was concerned about the center's "seat of the pants" management style. According to one United Way staff member, "Baxter didn't have a strategic plan and its internal record keeping was weak." Even more critically, United Way worried that Baxter's board operated too much in the shadow of Proctor.

It was not the first time United Way had expressed such concerns. For several years, its allocations committee had issued recommendations about Baxter's operations. Asked to present a strategic plan, Proctor would quickly crank out a two-page summary of his ideas. In the past, the United Way did not press hard. Baxter's day-care program was a success they could point to, and Proctor always got good press. Both Proctor and United Way recognized the value of the center as one of the few minority-run agencies that routinely received public praise. Proctor recalls that he was supremely confident the center would continue to receive United Way backing. But setting out to raise $1 million made United Way nervous. The fears were eventually quelled by members of the Business Advisory Committee who also happened to sit on the United Way board. United Way approved the capital campaign, but it continued to press Baxter to make management changes.

The capital campaign began formally in November 1988. The Business Advisory Committee, its members widely experienced in fund raising, had already drawn up a list of potential givers, estimated how much could be requested, and decided which committee member would make each contact. By early January 1989, Baxter had received $1 million in pledges. Within days, the sound of wrecking equipment could be heard. By September, the renovation was completed.

Raising $1 million in thirty days is a powerful testament to the trust and generosity of the Grand Rapids community. "Here," Proctor notes, "business is done with a handshake. There wasn't even a contract signed with the contractor." Contractor Dan Vos required each of his subcontractors to donate a minimum of 10 percent of their work; many donated more, some in excess of 50 percent. Donations from local furniture companies completed the interior decorating.

Baxter's once-crumbling school building now houses a spacious day-care facility, a medical and dental clinic staffed by six volunteer doctors and dozens of nurses, and ample offices for the staff. The new facility has had a very positive impact on staff morale, and tenant rents generate $30,000 yearly.

The Board Works

United Way's concerns about the center's internal management were heeded. Proctor acknowledges that at first he did not pay serious attention to the flaws United Way cited. The Baxter board had fallen into a comfortable pattern of letting Proctor run the show. Proctor now admits he was "scared to death of stronger board leadership." But in 1988, the board initiated a planning process. The head of the board asked member Candace Fluman, a respected hospital administrator, to chair the long-range planning committee. She was given charge of developing and implementing a strategic plan. Every effort was made to foster board and staff participation, so as to ensure a sense of ownership. With full board support, Fluman set about gathering as much information about the center as possible. She whirled through Baxter, conducting interviews and brainstorming sessions with staff, collecting data on programs, and meeting with board members. Her approach was data based. She reviewed a needs assessment of the Baxter area and the center's services that had been done by students from nearby Grand Valley State College. In addition to producing useful demographic information, the survey analyzed the center's existing programs and suggested new ones.

Fluman also reviewed the center's key organizational documents, from articles of incorporation and bylaws to financial records. She worked closely with Baxter's assistant director, Jim Talen. Despite antiquated technology, Talen had assembled the basics of a management information system. Together Talen and Fluman generated statistical profiles on each of Baxter's programs. To complete the data profile, a volunteer was recruited to survey similar agencies in the immediate area. Next came a half-day planning session with staff. The data were carefully introduced to provoke discussion of Baxter's strengths and weaknesses and areas of opportunity. It was the first time staff had ever met in such a session. According to one staff person, "It was exhilarating and empowering."

But the process was not over. Proctor was asked to summarize the program areas. Committee chairs provided descriptions of committee activities and prepared goal statements. A final report, including a long list of recommendations, was accepted by the board. The next objective was to produce a strategic plan. Fluman drafted a list of goals, action steps, and responsibilities. Top priority: have the board to develop a better understanding of its role. The strategic plan was drafted in August 1989 and adopted several months later.

Internal organizational changes quickly followed. In January 1990, United Way sponsored a half-day training program for Baxter's board; nineteen of the twenty-one members attended. Many learned, for the first time, about nonprofit boards: why they are important, what is expected, and how to fulfill responsibilities. In the past, Proctor explains, "the board was there to receive information and make observations." Sometimes, he adds, the board did not even have a quorum for meetings. "Now the board is more roll-up-the-sleeves," he says. New members have been recruited, including a lawyer (who is updating Baxter's bylaws), an accountant, and several human resource specialists. An effort is currently underway to recruit more minority members. A board manual is being assembled and an orientation program designed.

Proctor says he welcomes the changes. "They ultimately make my job easier," he says. United Way, too, approves. "In the past Gene would be in charge at Baxter's presentations to the allocations committee," says United Way's Nancy Ryan.

"Now it's the board." Ryan underscores, however, that the challenge ahead for Baxter is to make these board changes a habit.

Looking to the Future

Baxter still has areas that need work. Proctor's management style remains loose. He is strong on conveying values, impressing others with his industriousness and deeply held personal commitment, but structure seems anathema to him. Still, he can be tough and decisive. During his first month on the job in 1978, Proctor recalls, he fired thirteen employees funded by the federal Comprehensive Employment and Training Act. "They were doing absolutely nothing," he says. Such deliberate action alerted Baxter's remaining staff that this new boss would demand performance. Proctor has also nurtured extraordinary loyalty. Says Amway's Casey Wondergem: "Gene is humble, isn't macho, doesn't wear Brooks Brothers suits, knows how to deal with the Peninsula Club [the business executives' private club]—and never forgets the clients."

Proctor is ably assisted by Jim Talen, Baxter's assistant director. Talen has been the quiet insider while Proctor plays to the public. Talen's obsession with detail compensates for Proctor's gift for painting the big picture. Were Proctor to depart today, he would leave a grave leadership vacuum. Should Talen go, the center's day-to-day management would suffer. Baxter still has no organizational chart with clear lines of who reports to whom. Several among the staff and volunteers are profoundly religious and will challenge earthly authority with precepts such as "The Lord leads."

The good news is that Proctor and the board are increasingly sharing responsibilities. And the board is learning about internal management needs. It is working with staff to update job descriptions for the first time in over a decade. It is also reviewing personnel policies and evaluating each of the center's program areas. Job descriptions are being prepared for board members, an outgrowth of United Way's training program.

One near-term issue is to stabilize Baxter's funding. Although the center has three steady sources of funds in addition to United Way—church donations, fees for day care, and rent from tenants—some $43,500 in local government support is being jeopardized by a budget crunch. Proctor is considering seeking an endowment to ensure financial stability.

Baxter Community Center is a story of an agency being tested, and being strengthened as a result. It owes its survival to a special blend of riches—a sustaining Christian Reform Church, a charismatic leader and the hard-working loyalists on his staff, the beneficence of Grand Rapids's business community, and the gentle but persistent prodding of the local United Way, which helped convert a passive board into a bolder and more spirited body.

Chapter Seven

East Bay Asian
Local Development Corporation:
Entrepreneurship
at the Grass Roots

———————————◆—————————————

Excluding foundations, can you name one nonprofit organization that generates so much revenue that it makes charitable
donations? So many nonprofits live "grant-to-mouth" that the
concept of one being in a donor position seems extraordinary.
But that is precisely the situation that recently confronted the
East Bay Asian Local Development Corporation (EBALDC).

"Last year," says Lynette Lee, EBALDC's soft-spoken executive director, "our Asian Resource Center had more surplus
revenue from for-profit tenants than the IRS would allow us
as a nonprofit entity." EBALDC had a choice: donate the surplus to other charitable organizations, or pay taxes. The group
decided to give the money to the nonprofit tenants in its center.
"It's ironic," Lee observes. "While we make such donations, we
must raise funds for our own staff shortfalls."

EBALDC is a community-based development organization, dedicated to sparking development activity in the Chinatown neighborhood of Oakland, California. EBALDC acquires
and develops residential and commercial real estate; it also de-

51

livers social services such as health care, immigration assistance, and employment training.

In the fourteen years since its incorporation, EBALDC has grown from a fledgling group with a $25,000 grant from the San Francisco Foundation to a solid organization with over $8 million in assets. The group's flagship project, its Asian Resource Center, is a cavernous 73,000-square-foot property in the heart of Chinatown. EBALDC also rehabilitated and owns the Madrone Hotel. Decrepit and vacant for nine years, it now provides 32 clean, safe, rooms for very low-income tenants — elderly, formerly homeless, working poor, and disabled. By 1990 EBALDC expected to have another 119 apartments ready for occupancy, with commercial space and a public parking garage. That project, valued at $17 million, is the organization's most ambitious.

More than 2,000 community-based development organizations are currently operating in the United States. Regarded as a uniquely American phenomenon, they marry entrepreneurship with grassroots organizing. Though there is no formal scorecard, "EBALDC is up there in the golden 100, as its financials demonstrate, as well as its remaining true to the mission of helping the poor," says one observer.

For EBALDC, the goal of becoming self-sufficient, so elusive for most nonprofits, is on its way to becoming reality. But it was not always in such sound financial shape. And even with its strong track record, it is never easy to package multimillion-dollar deals for the people and neighborhoods EBALDC serves. But EBALDC is an exemplary nonprofit, with a clearly articulated mission and solid leadership. Its board, once insular and inexperienced, is now more diverse and provides sound, creative direction.

An Ambitious Idea

Oakland's Chinatown, neighbor to the comparatively affluent city of Berkeley, became a focus of activity two decades ago for Chinese student activists, many of whom had grown up there. In 1975, a group of students incorporated EBALDC with the goal of turning a vacant and deteriorated building, the largest in Chinatown, into a convalescent facility. The students had no track record. But with youthful energy, they approached the building's owners and asked them to donate it. Remarkably, the students were not dismissed. The owners offered them a purchase option — the students would have to come up with a down payment and a schedule for outright purchase.

The next step was a feasibility study. The students turned to their professors in the Asian Studies and Architecture Departments at the University of California at Berkeley. Asian, Inc., a community development corporation located across the bay in San Francisco, assisted. The study recommended that EBALDC shelve the convalescent project; it was too expensive. But from this process emerged another idea: turn the building into a multiservice center where the needs of the Asian population could be provided under one roof.

Even for experienced private companies, real estate development is complicated. For a novice nonprofit developer, the barriers were enormous. Financial institutions were not accustomed to working with EBALDC. None of the handful of other community development organizations in the Bay Area had ever tried anything quite like what the group was proposing.

Building a Savvy Board

EBALDC's young and inexperienced board of ten persisted. The Clorox Company Foundation, headquartered in Oakland, agreed to provide $5,000 to cover the down payment for the building. The San Francisco Foundation chipped in to fund two staffers, whose task it became to raise $2.5 million — the acquisition and development costs of the project.

"The board had energy, time, and [its members] were devoted," said a long-time friend of EBALDC. "But it didn't have contacts." The San Francisco Foundation, recalls Lee, "felt the board was really dragging." Henry Izumizaki, the foundation's program officer responsible for the project, remembers those early days, too. "The board in a project like that would have to provide the leadership, but it wasn't very mature." The San

Francisco Foundation, however, was itself in the midst of organizational change. "We were very conscious of growing pains," he says. "That experience gave us sensitivity, and so we were willing to pay for retreats, facilitators, and so forth." At one such retreat, EBALDC's board came to terms with its need to bring on a more experienced chair. The organization was on dead center for two years, and then in 1977, the deputy director of the Bay Area United Way became EBALDC's board chair.

One of the first concerns was recruitment of new board members. Because EBALDC's goal was to create a multiservice center, the initial board had brought in representatives from a variety of social services agencies, including prospective tenants. But this created conflicts: Rather than pushing the EBALDC agenda, they had their own. Other than stipulating that board members must be residents of Alameda or Contra Costa counties, EBALDC's bylaws gave no guidance on the matter of composition. "There was a growing recognition that individuals with particular skills and contacts would be better prepared to serve EBALDC's needs at that time," explains Lee. Under new stewardship, the board was soon reconstituted; the size was kept at ten, but more businesspeople and professionals were brought in.

During this tenuous period, EBALDC found an angel. Hugh Taylor, the local representative for the Economic Development Administration (a division of the U.S. Department of Commerce), agreed to provide EBALDC with funds to pay for the acquisition and part of the rehabilitation costs of its center. The next hurdle: to raise the rest of the money. The price tag for the multiservice center would eventually top $4 million.

Leaping Financial Burdens

Meanwhile, after years of decline, investment in Chinatown began to soar. The Asian population swelled with new immigrants and refugees. Lenders who would not touch Chinatown before were suddenly interested.

By late 1978, EBALDC and its reconstituted board had successfully tapped several public and private sources for operating support. But it still was a fragile organization. The core staff of two was supplemented by workers funded under the federal government's Comprehensive Employment and Training Act. A handful of consultants worked for very modest fees.

Though EBALDC had made headway, it was far from its goal. Fortunately, a few funders were patient. "Development, in both the organizational as well as real estate sense, takes years," says Izumizaki. "We [the San Francisco Foundation] were naive and willing to experiment." The William and Flora Hewlett Foundation also became one of EBALDC's early boosters.

Soon, word of EBALDC's efforts spread throughout the small network of community economic development funders. The Ford Foundation, after a site visit, made a $737,000 loan, on the condition that a private lender participate on an equal basis. Two years later, sufficient financing was finally secured and the rehabilitation proceeded. In late 1980, the first tenants moved in. Organizations serving Asians were first. But EBALDC's troubles were not over.

Its balance sheet was predicated on filling all three floors of the center with a mix of for-profit tenants. Funds for finishing the third-floor renovations had not been raised yet. Part of EBALDC's unique ideology was that nonprofits would pay concessionary rates—below market-rate rents. Shortly after the first tenants moved in, EBALDC faced an operating-cost shortfall and nearly failed to make its loan payments. But EBALDC refused to change the center's tenant mix or squeeze its occupants for more rent.

Lynette Lee, who became EBALDC's executive director in 1982, immediately set about to tackle the delicate financial situation. She examined the books and management practices. To her horror, Lee discovered one tenant had withheld $8,000 in rent over a $500 dispute. She personally took over the property management, thus eliminating the fee for a management firm. The space plan was reassessed. The retail configuration was made smaller, and EBALDC sold off an adjacent parcel, which netted almost $170,000.

Working at a feverish pace, Lee applied to the Office of Community Services (U.S. Department of Health and Human Services) for a grant to ready the third floor for occupancy.

EBALDC was awarded $250,000, finished the rehabilitation in 1984, and brought in a division of the state of California Department of Social Services as the center's anchor tenant. The project had taken nearly ten years.

Fine Tuning the Organization

By 1985, EBALDC's baling wire and adhesive tape phase was over. The organization had a strong and well-organized board, a respected chair, a no-nonsense executive director, and a track record. Lee's eyes twinkle as she notes that "the Asian Resource Center is two-thirds equity." EBALDC's financial statement would be the envy of many a small business.

Lee has been at EBALDC almost from the beginning. She came aboard with a college degree in English literature and a teaching credential. She had no formal training in real estate or business development. But as executive director, she has overseen most of EBALDC's stunning development successes. Self-effacing and predisposed to shyness, Lee does not fit the conventional image of a big-time developer. "She's not the fire and brimstone Knute Rockne type," says Henry Isumizaki. "But in her quiet, understated way, she gets the job done."

Above all, Lee is a community entrepreneur, fighting for the needs of the poor. EBALDC's success could tempt it to stray from its mission, but this has not happened. The reason is the clarity and purposefulness of the board and executive director, neither of whom has forgotten the organization's humble beginnings.

Internally, Lee has worked with her board to strengthen its structure. Though the board had come a long way from the wide-eyed group of students, in 1982 it was time for a mileage check. The board held a retreat — and has every year since — to revisit the mission and clarify board roles. As a result of that first retreat, EBALDC changed its board composition to incorporate representatives from Oakland's increasingly diverse Asian population, including Cambodians, Laotians, Vietnamese, and Koreans. The organization expanded its mission to include housing and business development, plus advocacy. It established a five-year plan.

"Because we had professionals on the board," reflects Lee, "we put financial and personnel systems in place relatively early on." Jack Chu, the current board chair, is a certified public accountant. Involved with EBALDC since its founding, Chu helped produce a manual detailing the organization's entire financial system. The *Internal Control System* manual, about fifty pages long, specifies management procedures, disbursements, check signing, the chart of accounts, and much more. This document establishes high standards and sends a signal of seriousness.

Putting together strong personnel policies required more resources. Lee turned to a local management assistance center. Combining its advice with a few borrowed manuals and her own good instincts, Lee wrote the personnel policies herself. "Personnel policies, of course, didn't teach me to be a manager,"she says. That was much tougher.

Leadership in an Ethnic Culture

"I didn't know how to delegate and had to learn to do so," Lee explains. "I have a tendency to hire strong people with a lot of initiative." EBALDC's staffing has always been skeletal, never exceeding about five full-timers. Shortly after she became director, Lee disagreed with one staff member, who complained to other staff and the board. "I learned through that experience that I can't risk being circumspect and that it's more humane to be direct with staff," she says.

For Lee, learning to assert herself was very difficult. "I was raised by my grandmother, who taught me and my siblings to be quiet and deferential," she observes. "As an Asian woman, I not only had to work through my own generally shy and quiet personality, but also being a woman without formal training in real estate and development. So many times," Lee says, "I have been the only female in a development meeting. Fortunately that is changing."

Tom Lauderbach, EBALDC's development specialist, notes that "Lee brings in some very strong people who will argue long and hard. The negative is you get no space. The positive is knowing she pushes hard on the outside and will never send staff into the flames." Lauderbach is a technician, familiar with the jargon and numerical mumbo-jumbo of real estate development. Lee is the generalist. But she has an ample understanding of real estate, and plenty of street smarts and experience. She has polished her real estate skills at the Development Training Institute, a national nonprofit that specializes in training community development leaders.

EBALDC's staff and board have fused a strong relationship with their community. Francis SamSotha, a Cambodian refugee and EBALDC board member, believes EBALDC's board "is the tops in mix, understanding, and commitment." SamSotha runs a nonprofit that helps refugees get resettled. Other board members, mostly Chinese, are successful professionals — accountants, lawyers, and businesspeople. Tensions can run high between Asian cultures and could be exacerbated by so diverse a board, but they are minimized at EBALDC. "The reason for this," SamSotha neatly summarizes, "is we know EBALDC is for everyone. It's ours."

Looking Ahead

In 1987, as its first five-year plan came to a close, EBALDC put in motion the development of another. At that time, the organization reaffirmed its goals and purpose. Today, EBALDC is at a threshold. Thanks to the success of its Asian Resource Center and its entry into other development activities, the organization is poised for more and larger projects. Others approach with ideas. "The challenge for EBALDC," says Henry Izumizaki, "is to have strategy and to anticipate change."

EBALDC is trying to do just that. It recently received a grant from the Ford Foundation to hire a planner to do a comprehensive needs assessment covering external as well as internal needs. The grant proposal identifies a process that includes revisiting the group's vision, setting forth goals and objectives for the next five years, laying out a strategic plan, and stipulating community review. Throughout, various stakeholders — board members, staff, the community-at-large — will be involved.

Above all, EBALDC has a steadiness of purpose. It knows that the bottom line is not the numbers on the real estate pro forma, but the difference that this exemplary group has made for the people it serves.

Chapter Eight

Guadalupe Center:
Leadership That Heals

———————•———————

Kansas City—the city of barbecued ribs, stockyards, and roaring jazz—is also the home of one of the largest Mexican populations in the United States. In the aftermath of the revolution of 1910, Mexicans in search of a better life moved across the border to follow harvests and work on railroads or in the packing houses.

Today, an estimated 60,000 Hispanics live in Kansas City. To serve their needs, Guadalupe Center was founded six decades ago by a group of white female volunteers from the Catholic church. Today, the center is an independent advocacy organization run by Hispanics, with a staff of twenty and a $600,000 budget.

For many residents, Guadalupe Center is a lifeline. In a recent survey, 92 percent of Missouri Hispanics interviewed rated the center as "very important." So too did 79 percent of the leaders interviewed and 96 percent of local human service agencies representatives.

The center's multiple services range from day care, preschool education, and tutoring to programs to improve literacy,

59

award college scholarships, and promote parent involvement. Guadalupe's bimonthly newspaper keeps constituents informed. The center tends the homeless, supplies food and companionship to the elderly, and is an advocate for immigrants. Its programs are spread among four buildings. Its mission is clear and well defined, its resources stable. But the one characteristic of this exemplary nonprofit that immediately stands out is its leadership development. Guadalupe Center excels in promoting personal and professional development for its staff and the people they serve.

Church Beginnings

The first Mexican settlers in Kansas City were not especially welcomed. Discrimination and poor English skills blocked their access to good jobs. The city was slow to respond. In 1919, a Catholic women's club converted a church originally built by the Swedish Lutherans into a volunteer school and clinic in the West Side neighborhood where many of the new immigrants had settled. With a few picture changes and a new altar, it became Kansas City's Church of Our Lady of Guadalupe and the first home of Guadalupe Center, one of the nation's oldest social service agencies serving Hispanics.

According to John Duncan, a long-time member of Guadalupe's board and also its historian, "Miss Dorothy Gallagher was responsible for turning the center from a band of volunteers into an agency with staff and programs." Dubbed the "fairy godmother" of Kansas City's Mexican colony, Gallagher and her family provided three cottages for the center's activities in the 1920s. Funding from the Heart of America United Way, starting in 1924, provided essential stabilizing support. By 1936, the Mexican population and Guadalupe's programs had grown so large that Gallagher built a structure to house everything under one roof.

From its inception, the center was tied to the local Catholic diocese. Gallagher reported directly to the church. There was no community participation in decision making; indeed, there was no real board through which the community could communicate. The center incorporated independently in 1946, but the bishop was automatically the chair of its board and had ultimate authority. The church was Guadalupe's anchor for half a century. By 1974, however, it had become an albatross.

That year, the center's peaceful coexistence with the diocese turned sour over the hiring of a new executive director. The bishops did not approve of the director that Guadalupe's board had chosen. The board was divided. "Hispanics are taught not to fight authority, let alone the authority of the church," explains Chris Medina, executive director. "The board came back asking the bishop for a reason. He said he didn't need to give any."

The board decided to sever ties with the church, and matters turned messy. The bishop ousted the center from the diocese property. He tried to prevent Guadalupe Center from using its name. And he went to United Way, specifically to apply for the very funding that was the center's lifeline.

Wounded but also galvanized, the board and staff fought back. They found a new site and retained the Guadalupe Center name. United Way agreed to stick with them. Those dollars, plus the United Way imprimatur, played a vital role in keeping the Guadalupe Center alive. In the fifteen years since that turbulent rift with the church, Guadalupe's budget has grown more than tenfold. United Way remains a key supporter.

Cultivating Leaders

"I grew up in the Westside, and in a way grew up at the center," says Medina, who has headed Guadalupe since 1980. As a youth, he participated in the center's activities, and eventually worked in various capacities—as recreation leader, day camp director, and bookkeeper. "Chris was groomed from the outset to take my place," says Tony Salazar, who preceded Medina as executive director. Succession was very smooth.

Staff, funders, and board members describe Medina as hardworking, tenacious, persistent, and dedicated. "Integrity" and "commitment" are two other characteristics they mention frequently. Medina is a role model for his staff and for the larger community.

Chris's philosophy is that we give something back to our

community, make a contribution," says Bernardo Ramirez, Guadalupe's assistant director. Medina actively nurtures staff leadership capabilities not only by serving as a role model, but by hiring initiators, delegating responsibilities, providing an environment where people feel free to ask for assistance, and encouraging networking and community involvement. Attracting dedicated staff is relatively easy. "They find us," says Medina. Many come from the Westside, a neighborhood of about 7,500, about half of whom are Hispanic. Staff turnover is minimal.

Medina has a special talent for spotting, and then capitalizing on, an individual's strengths. Confessed Ramirez: "I'm a good example of someone who was already brushing up against the wrong side of the law. Chris's faith in me put me on the right side." Medina responds: "Bernardo was much more good than bad. He just needed someone to believe in him." With Medina's encouragement, Ramirez blossomed. Once a college dropout, he is now attending community college, thanks to Guadalupe's policy of giving six hours off each week for formal education. Ramirez was first hired as an emergency assistance counselor. He worked in several other capacities until Medina promoted him to assistant director. He is a potential successor to Medina.

Medina is also an excellent delegator. "Each program is run relatively independently, and directors are responsible for hiring staff and for proposal writing," he explains. Though some have never had these responsibilities, "you're not afraid to ask for help," says Gilbert Guerrero, Guadalupe's education director.

Assistance has come from many sources. The National Council of La Raza (Guadalupe Center is an affiliate) provides information, training, and essential linkages to the network of Hispanic service providers. La Raza arranged for Ramirez to do an internship in Washington, D.C., where he learned policy analysis and became an expert on immigration law. The center also receives support from the local nonprofit management assistance center, board members, and from one of Kansas City's premier corporations, Hallmark Cards. A corporate volunteer from Hallmark has been working with Guadalupe's senior staff to build their strategic planning capabilities.

Staff members are formally evaluated once a year by their immediate supervisors and by Medina, who acknowledges a weakness — not complimenting staff enough. "He's like a father, makes you feel part of a family, but isn't quick with praise," said one staff member. "My father was a professional soccer player and made the World Cup team," Medina responds. "He taught me not to get big-headed, to stay in reality, and be an example. Others will do the talking." But Medina is learning he should do more talking, too.

An Active Board

From its founding in 1919 until 1974, Guadalupe's passive board obeyed the dictates of the diocese. The breakup with the church, says former director Salazar, "led to an extremely aggressive board, to the point of becoming somewhat intrusive." Today, Guadalupe has a strong working board.

Medina's personal style, encouraging collaboration, contributes to the board's strength. Good attendance and participation are the norm for the twenty-four members. "We look for committed people who are willing to invest their time helping us achieve the mission," says board chair Rita Botello. Board members' common bonds are readily evident: in shared family values, education, and the desire to help others. Though Guadalupe is nonsectarian, religion also seems a part of the bond.

Guadalupe is a grassroots organization. To ensure its ear is close to the ground, half of the board positions are reserved for Westside residents. For the remaining members, Medina says, "we look for where we have needs and look to ensure representativeness." In recent years, Guadalupe has been recruiting professionals, including accountants, lawyers, corporate executives, and others who could be instrumental in fund raising.

A board member's term is three years. Terms are staggered to bring in new blood, but there are no limits on the number of terms that can be served. John Duncan has been on the board for more than twenty years. Many others, too, have served multiple terms. But Guadalupe's board has escaped a problem common to many nonprofits: accumulating members who do not participate fully but are not removed. It's tempting to attribute good board attendance to the warning in the center's bylaws: "Any director who has three consecutive unexcused absences from regular meetings of the Board of Directors may be replaced." But other groups have similar proscriptions that go unheeded. "If someone calls beforehand to excuse themself because of a conflict, that's okay," explains Medina. "But we did have to vote out someone who repeatedly missed meetings without explanation."

The incentive to attend — not the threat of penalty — brings people to Guadalupe's monthly meetings. "In the past, it's helped that this is a small community so we know each other," explains board chair Botello. Five new members were brought aboard in 1989, when the center had its first formal orientation. Board members, Medina, and the staff gave an overview of programs. Each new member was invited to visit the facilities. Most already had.

A Broader Mission

In 1988, Guadalupe contracted with the local management assistance center to train its board. Bylaws and personnel policies were reviewed. Eventually, Guadalupe's mission was reviewed, a process that Medina acknowledges was overdue. Originally focused only on the Westside neighborhood, the center found itself spreading out into other parts of the city as the Hispanic community expanded. Guadalupe was sensitive to potential turf wars.

"The needs brought us into other places, and we are able to serve them," Medina says. In the late 1970s a concerted effort was made to pour resources into the center "rather than spreading monies across many groups," adds Salazar. "Guadalupe was already positioned to get the job done," Salazar says. Guadalupe recast its mission to encompass the larger metropolitan area, but retains Westside as its primary service area.

Resource Development

In the past, the center was preoccupied with the constant uphill battle for resources and handling the split with Guadalupe

Parish. "Chris has worked to mend that relationship. He is a collaborative type and is seen as a healer," says board member Bob Reed, an executive with the local utility company. The two organizations recently began planning joint educational activities. With the mission clear and the unpleasant history behind them, Reed says, "the board is able to concentrate on resource development and stabilization."

The center's funding grew fivefold over the 1980s. "Chris has developed into a topnotch fund raiser," says Reed. Virtually every possible mechanism for funding is used — from foundations, corporations, and government to fees for services, special events, membership dues, and individual donations. More than half the budget comes from public funds, mostly from the federal government. "We've gotten very aggressive about finding requests for proposals and have gotten better at competing," Medina says. The center also taps city and state resources, particularly for education programs targeted to minorities.

Monies from United Way — about $132,000 annually — constitute less than 20 percent of the Guadalupe budget, but have been vital in keeping the group alive. The philanthropy recently shifted from agency to program funding. As a result, specific Guadalupe activities, such as day care, now receive the support. Guadalupe has "a committed board, long history, and solid track record," says Diane Powell, United Way liaison to the center. "We've asked them to pay more attention to certain areas," she adds, "including strategic planning, program planning, and evaluation." Too often, Powell confesses, "with social service agencies we're relying on gut feeling and a belief that we'd know if the constituency was displeased."

Donations have also flowed to the center from the Greater Kansas City Community Foundation, Hallmark Cards, Hall Family Foundation, Gannett Outdoor Company, Xerox, and IBM. Some companies participate in apprenticeship programs; corporate volunteers are also part of the center's tutorial corps. Foundation and corporate donations are about 20 percent of Guadalupe's budget.

Guadalupe's one major fund-raising event, a food and entertainment festival known as "Fiesta Hispaña," is held each year during Spanish Heritage Week. Sponsored jointly with other

Hispanic groups, the fiesta attracted more than 40,000 people in 1988. The night before the event, the center hosts an annual awards banquet to honor board members, volunteers, and students who have won scholarships. It is a formal, black-tie dinner. The event, says Medina, is "meant to make a statement about our successes." A working committee, comprising Medina, board members, and volunteers, plan the fiesta. A local distributor provides beer, cups, and a small monetary contribution. Guadalupe sells the beer — and netted about $9,000 in 1988. Monies from the sale of soda pop are set aside for a local Hispanic youth group. Each division of Guadalupe is encouraged to participate. Typically, the elderly programs, school, and other Guadalupe activities operate their own booths.

Membership dues and fees for services also add to the center's treasury. But, says Medina, these are very small, "since we know we can't ask for much." A plan to raise more money from individuals is on the drawing board, but much of that will likely be directed first to the new Hispanic Development Fund, a local organization that provides grants to organizations like Guadalupe Center.

The Guadalupe board recognizes that despite all the new monies and local generosity, it cannot rest on its laurels. In the discussion stage are plans to establish a corporate advisory committee. Bob Reed, familiar with similar board satellite groups, is taking the lead. Both Reed and Medina know the difficulties in getting top-level corporate involvement, especially in securing time commitments. They are trying to carefully focus their requests to corporate leaders.

A corporate advisory panel could bring new recognition, contacts, and funding. It could allow the center to experiment and provide added services. But such a group will not relieve Guadalupe of the typical nonprofit's burden: raising adequate funding to provide for the needs of a population unable to pay for services.

Past as Prologue: Into the 1990s

Guadalupe Center is part of the rhythm of life for Kansas City's Westside, and increasingly so for other residents throughout the city. Every day a van transports elderly people to Casa Feliz where they eat, socialize, and get help with their problems. Children pour into the day-care and special bilingual education programs; youth can be found in the gym after school or receiving guidance to improve their proficiency in reading, computers, and other skills.

For the college bound, the Hispanic Development Fund offers a chance to win scholarships. Created in 1986 with a gift from the Hall Family Foundation, the fund awarded over $50,000 in scholarships in 1989 and received matching monies for the awardees from most local colleges and universities.

For the Mexican families who crossed the border at the start of the twentieth century, Guadalupe Center meant a place of caring, where they could renew their faith in themselves and in others, where they could reaffirm their decision to come to a new land in search of greater opportunities. For their children and grandchildren, and for newcomers, Guadalupe Center has not changed. One priority is to keep the West Side community intact. At one time, the neighborhood had more than 20,000 residents, but freeways eventually reduced its population to 7,500. Situated in the shadow of Kansas City's illustrious Crown Center (the hotel, office, and shopping complex built by Hallmark), West Side today attracts speculators. The threat is not immediate, but Medina sees potential encroachment looming on the horizon. Looking to the future, he says, "we've built our advocacy skills, and will make every effort to keep this community intact." Breaking up the Westside would decimate the Hispanic enclave, but Guadalupe Center stands a good chance of holding its ground.

Chapter Nine

Indian Health Board:
Challenging the Status Quo

———————————◆·◆———————————

Norine Smith, who directs the Indian Health Board (IHB) in Minneapolis, had never heard of Saul Alinsky when she brought her staff members and their children to disrupt a board meeting of the local community development agency. But she knew instinctively how to employ the renowned Chicago organizer's aggressive tactics. "Certain promises had been made to the board and I wanted to make sure they remembered," Smith says. In case agency officials missed the point, Smith and IHB's assistant director, Joanne Barr, poked at them with umbrellas. Smith, by the way, got what she wanted.

Smith is an American Indian (as is Barr). But fellow Indians have sometimes branded her an "apple"—red on the surface but white inside. Others have heckled and harassed. Smith's transgression is that she forthrightly confronts a central problem in the Indian community—alcoholism. She is unwavering in her determination to "get Indians to confront their destructive behavior patterns and to prove that they can do quality work." This message, along with Smith's own deeply embedded drive to succeed, makes the Indian Health Board much more than the "primary health care facility" described in its bylaws and annual reports. But it is also why the organization's mission gets a little blurry and why management and personnel problems have erupted periodically over IHB's seventeen-year history.

IHB's story is one of challenging norms, of befriending powerful legislators, of getting a law through Congress, and winning a grant to become a "model" Indian health center for the nation. In time, there would be over thirty similar health boards nationwide. Today, IHB provides medical, dental, mental health, and an array of social services. In a typical year, its professionals handle more than 20,000 medical and dental appointments. The agency also receives special funding for youth leadership programs.

Once, clients lacking transportation were brought to IHB in so-called Indian cars — known for breaking down. Now they are ferried to and from the clinic in IHB's own vehicles. Medicaid or Medicare covers the cost of treating the poor and elderly; those who can, pay on a sliding scale.

IHB has a staff of more than sixty and an annual budget of around $2 million. In 1971 the budget was $150,000, derived entirely from a federal grant. Today, IHB receives a mix of resources from government, third-party payers, foundations, and individuals. Its growth, ups and downs, and increasing professionalism offer a telling story of ethnic leadership in tumultuous times.

From Advocacy to Health Care

Just as it was for society at large, the decade of the 1960s was a turning point for American Indians. Fresh leaders surfaced, longstanding problems were identified, and new organizations formed. Smith, who was born and raised on Minnesota's Red Lake Indian Reservation before moving to Minneapolis, found herself "going to lots of community meetings," she says. She did not really consider herself an activist, but she was part of a loose network of people interested in improving health care for Indians.

Smith joined a local leader named Charlie Deegan (who would eventually become IHB's first director) in requesting help from Senator Hubert H. Humphrey and Representative Don Fraser. The two influential Minnesota lawmakers gave Deegan and Smith a crash course in shepherding a bill through Congress. Community leaders did their part. The result: a nationwide demonstration project on Indian health. IHB became the first site funded under the new law. Deegan, who by then had gained some notoriety, found himself in demand around the country. Meanwhile, back in Minneapolis, IHB would find itself modifying its initial vision within six months.

Based on initial survey information, IHB began as an advocacy organization. It hired Indians to help others get proper medical services, typically at hospital emergency rooms, and to make sure Indians "didn't fall through the cracks of an alien system," Smith says. With a federal award of $150,000, and more thorough surveying and follow-up, IHB determined it could better serve the Indian population by establishing its own primary health care facility.

This was an enormous leap. Special physical space would be required, along with expensive equipment and, of course, doctors. Smith, who was then IHB's office manager, took on the task with gusto. With the help of Joanne Barr, she found, of all places, a former morgue. Their first office, Smith says, was "the room where they used to draw blood from the bodies."

To transform the morgue into clinical space, Smith turned to a friend in the construction business. It was to be the first of many times Smith would invoke her special talents for knowing when and how to seek outside help. The builder taught Smith and several other Indian women basic carpentry. Plumbing and electrical services were paid for by a local foundation. Materials were in short supply, so Smith called on the "plywood king of Minnesota"—Rudy Boschwitz, who later became U.S. Senator. Ready with truck and trailer, Smith was soon at his door to pick up plywood, cabinets, and insulation, all free of charge.

Getting medical equipment was the next hurdle. A brainstorm led Smith and Barr to ask local hospitals for lists of retired physicians. With truck and trailer again at the ready, the two women found physicians who would donate their used equipment in exchange for a nice tax deduction. "We got a lot of real museum-quality stuff," Smith explains, "but we got what we needed, too." An unexpected longer-term payoff, she notes, was the publicity. News of this band of gutsy Indian women hauling medical equipment provided great gossip — and some technical assistance, too.

Meanwhile, IHB staff were feverishly writing proposals to get funding for a doctor. After forty-nine unsympathetic no's, a yes came from the Donner Foundation in New York, and in 1973, IHB's primary health care facility opened. In barely two years, IHB's dedicated band of activists, short on funds and contacts but long on dreams and determination, had pulled off a monumental achievement.

Within the community, the need for health care was so acute that no advertising was needed. Indians were soon queuing up to see IHB's doctor and dentist. But even while success was swift, problems began to emerge inside the organization.

Indian "Corporate Culture"

IHB's leaders knew little about writing papers of incorporation or bylaws, and had no experience working with a board. Charlie Deegan, the executive director, had never run an organization. The rudimentary bylaws called for a board of twenty-four; the prime concern was to ensure that each tribe was represented.

The new trustees were unfamiliar with board roles and responsibilities. There was no orientation, no policy manual, no guidance on how to become a working board. Deegan controlled, recalls Smith. "He believed in the mission, was bullheaded and with an unsophisticated board got his way." Deegan increasingly became a public figure, going to other cities and consulting on Indian health matters. When Deegan left IHB in 1976, Smith became acting director. She believes the board made the position "acting" because its members felt she would fail. In retrospect, Smith says, the board's decision was helpful because she felt she had nothing to lose.

Smith proceeded to launch a revolution. "Sloppy work practices had been permitted," she says. "People didn't come to work and still expected to get paid. There was favoritism, and internal controls were not existent." Not to mention a deficit. To Smith, IHB's internal workings represented the worst of "Indian corporate culture." She vowed to change things.

Her first step was to rewrite personnel policies: Employees would be paid only for time spent working; unexplained absenteeism would result in termination. Smith's bravado set off a wave of protests. Some staff members who were regularly skipping work had relatives on IHB's board. Some board members felt they could fight the new personnel rules because hiring and firing workers was not clearly delegated to the IHB executive director. Eventually, Smith prevailed. Time clocks and attendance requirements were introduced, as was a new restriction on relatives of board members being on the IHB staff. The executive director's power to hire and fire was clearly set forth.

Meanwhile, the IHB board was getting smaller through attrition. Smith and Barr redesigned the structure of the board, eventually reducing its size from twenty-four members to nine. They believed a smaller board would minimize turf battles and reduce board interference in IHB's day-to-day operations.

Putting Systems in Place

Smith's first two years at IHB, from 1976 to 1978, proved to be a watershed. In addition to the new personnel policies, IHB launched a new patient billing system. IHB senior staff and the board worked to sort out their respective responsibilities. And IHB's entire accounting system was targeted for cleanup. Smith again used her ample skills for getting assistance. From an earlier contact made at a Junior League meeting, where she had given a presentation on Indian culture, she recruited the *pro bono* assistance of the president of one of Minnesota's largest accounting firms. "The records were a disaster," she says. The accountants taught IHB how to do bookkeeping.

By 1978, new procedures had been initiated throughout IHB, from the board and staff to accounting. But the organization was outgrowing its space. Ellie Webster, one of IHB's first employees, suggested moving the clinic to an Indian housing project that was about to be foreclosed by the U.S. Department of Housing and Urban Development. IHB could meet its own space needs, Webster reasoned, and perhaps save the project from abandonment by becoming a reliable paying tenant.

But IHB at the time had a budget deficit. Should an organization having trouble enough keeping itself afloat take on an added burden? With her typical blind faith, Smith thought so. And the board agreed. Community Development Block Grant monies, among other sources, financed renovation of part of the housing project into a medical clinic.

The move, however, placed IHB in a dangerous setting. The housing project was run by the American Indian Movement (AIM), and "apples" like Smith and Barr were not always welcome. Smith and Barr joined the board of the housing project. They immediately found many of the same management problems that had earlier plagued IHB. When the two women protested, AIM threatened them. "We left meetings together, to make sure one would look behind so there wouldn't be any surprises," Smith says. "They brought their thugs, dressed in berets and wearing eyeshades, and thought they'd intimidate us." They failed.

IHB's internal systems were working smoothly and the deficit was slowly being wiped out. But the environment was wrecking the organization. "Our board chair attended a housing project board meeting and felt that it was too dangerous for us to stay," Smith remembers. "He made a recommendation to look for a new space."

So Smith scouted local hospitals. IHB, she reasoned, needed a location where patients could easily be referred. She struck a deal with Fairview Deaconess Hospital, whose bed counts, like many others in the area, were down. Smith used the promise of patient referrals to exact an agreement from the hospital to lease land at the concessionary rate of $100 annually for sixty-nine years. By this time a cash reserve had accumulated, and IHB built its own facility. By late 1983, IHB occupied a brand-new clinic.

IHB operated on a steady course for the next two years, but the peace was not to last. In 1985 Smith decided to computerize IHB's bookkeeping system. The clinic's lifeline was third-party billings — reimbursements paid by the government for medical services provided to Medicaid and Medicare patients, who were poor and elderly. Computerizing the accounting procedures, Smith reasoned, would track and speed payments. Smith went to the same major firm that had helped IHB revise its accounting system years earlier and was now handling the organization's books. "Unfortunately the firm had just undergone a merger," Smith recalls. "And we found ourselves lost in the shuffle." The company, she continues, "recommended hardware that was too small and software too old." The results were unfortunate. After working for years to successfully wipe out an earlier deficit, IHB now confronted a new budget shortfall of about $300,000. These were revenues anticipated from patient billings that the system failed to account.

The blow to IHB was serious. The group sued to recoup the money it had paid for the computer system and had lost from patient revenues. According to Smith, "The court settlement awarded us the hard money to pay for buying another system, but soft money to pay for the deficit was lost." The award came in 1987. Smith estimates it "will take probably to mid-1990 to fully recover."

The Winds of Change

Stability continues to elude IHB. Fairview Deaconess Hospital is closing, and Smith had to seek another referral arrangement. The land lease remains in effect, so IHB need not move again. Even so, IHB is outgrowing its present space. In addition to its medical, dental, and counseling services, the organization runs a large social service program, targeted principally to Indian children. The idea, says Smith, is "to get at the preventive side of alcoholism." Services range from tutoring to cultural activities. Smith believes the programs should have their own building.

With her usual entrepreneurial flair, Smith secured the

services of a volunteer to carry out a space analysis and determine what would be required for a capital campaign. IHB is also talking with the city's parks and recreation department about building a facility in a Minneapolis mini-park. IHB would finance the construction, while the land and building maintenance would remain the city's responsibility.

Changes at IHB's staff and board have also been in the works. In 1989, Smith's long-time associate Joanne Barr, took another job. As of mid-year, the position was not filled, which means that Smith pays even more attention to internal administration. "Several people could move in, but need more seasoning," she says. Indeed, IHB's most serious danger is its uncertain capacity to sustain itself should Smith leave.

IHB's consumer-based board, once overactive to the point of interfering with the staff, is now largely staff driven. Though IHB has been an affiliate of the local United Way since 1983, only recently have board members shown an active interest in United Way–sponsored training. "The training has moved them from rubber stamping decision making to taking on more responsibility and showing initiative," Smith says.

But such major responsibilities as fund raising are likely to remain Smith's job. Because the board is made up of active patients at the clinic, its members are typically not well connected or knowledgeable about the world of raising money. Smith has jumped into the vacuum. She does not foresee the board's assuming a fund-raising role. Instead, Smith is shifting that responsibility to staff. Some have resisted. As one middle manager put it: "Our programs were cut to the bone because of the deficit. And now we're expected to become proposal writers — which is like singing for our supper." But Smith is unrelenting. The board is not positioned to go after support, she says, and she cannot do everything.

Smith's immediate future goal, she says, is "to get out of debt and generate a positive cash flow." She is confident this can be achieved, thanks to greater efficiencies in patient billing.

In its early stages IHB was an outer-directed organization, preoccupied with being heard. Today, it is increasingly inner oriented, concerned with stabilizing its management and financial structures as well as its programs. IHB's strength, one local funder commented, "is Norine's profound concern for her people and her ability to take their case convincingly to policymakers and funders." So far, IHB has found its way through the storm clouds, thanks largely to its strong and entrepreneurial executive director.

With tiredness in her voice, Smith reflects: "I want to manage in a noncrisis mode. I don't want to be building anything."

Chapter Ten

Interlochen
Center for the Arts:
Unswerving Dedication
to Mission

————————◆————————

It is 6:45 A.M. A trumpet player rings in the summer morning with reveille, as a chorus of girls chants: "You gotta get up. You gotta get up." These are the sweet sounds of adolescents awakening the troops at Interlochen. And the music, art, dance and theater never stop—until taps.

Nestled deep in the woods of northern Michigan is the Interlochen Center for the Arts and its three legs: the National Music Camp, the Interlochen Arts Academy, and radio station WIAA, one of the best subscribed public stations in the nation. The music camp, founded in 1927, provides intensive training each summer to more than 2,000 talented youngsters, aged eight to eighteen, from all over the world. The camp sponsors more than 450 performing arts events every year. The Arts Academy, a year-round school founded in 1962, has an equally impressive record. Some 94 percent of its graduates go on to college, and 11 percent of all presidential scholars in the arts nationwide have come from its ranks. The center's annual budget exceeds $15.5 million. Over the past decade, it has a solid record of fiscal stability.

It was not always so. Not long ago, financial problems nearly closed Interlochen. The bustling youngsters toting instruments and art supplies twice their size created a positive public image, but privately, affairs at Interlochen were far from harmonious.

Interlochen's story is one of great vision, grand leadership, and ultimately sound management. But like many effective nonprofits, its path has had detours. After the center's charismatic founder, Joe Maddy, died, Interlochen's mission was sorely tested. The organization survived thanks to the unswerving dedication to mission on the part of its board members. Interlochen sustained other challenges, too. At one time, recruiting board members was more casual than strategic, and board capacity more latent than real. Today, Interlochen is a much stronger organization than it has ever been.

Leader of the Band

A half century ago, Joe Maddy had a dream. He wanted to create a world-class center for training young people in the performing arts. He began by launching the national music camp, today one of the foremost in the world. But there were problems along the way. In the beginning, the camp's relationship with nearby Traverse City, Michigan, was shaky. There were problems with local unions. Bills went unpaid. But Maddy—brilliant, arrogant, and mercurial—persisted, and the camp began to prosper.

By the 1960s, Maddy wanted to expand. He proposed creating a year-round arts academy at Interlochen. Fearing the endeavor would be financially unsound, the board disapproved. Interlochen's irrepressible founder pushed ahead anyway. According to an often-repeated story, when the board turned down Maddy's request, he responded: "I am going to go it alone." And he did.

Maddy found a corporate sponsor, W. Clement Stone, to finance the Interlochen Arts Academy. But from the start, just as the board feared, the school was a financial drain. There were tensions with the music camp. Some complaints were relatively minor. Students at the academy, camp officials charged, did not take proper care of musical instruments. Other strains were more serious. The camp, its directors charged, was being milked like a cash cow to keep the fiscally unstable academy going.

With Maddy in charge, Interlochen's leadership was strong, but there were virtually no management policies, no job descriptions, contracts, or performance evaluations. The board was largely passive. Maddy spent money the way he wanted to, never worrying about the bills. Financial management was almost nonexistent; resource development governed largely by serendipity. Interlochen was Maddy's own personal enterprise, and, according to those who knew him, the founder had no patience for people who did not toe his line.

In 1966, Maddy died, and Interlochen entered a turbulent phase. Interlochen's board was ill equipped for the transition and fell into disarray. Many board members, hand picked by Maddy, had served for well over a decade. But the board had been consistently shielded from information about Interlochen's operations. Though profoundly dedicated to the organization's mission, the board was unprepared to carry out its responsibilities effectively.

Turbulent Times

After Maddy's death, the board appointed a three-member committee to hold down the fort during the search for a successor. Aware of Interlochen's serious financial debts, board members instinctively looked for a prominent person who could raise funds. In 1968, the board hired a well-known radio personality to take Maddy's job. The marriage soon ended in divorce. The new president, it turned out, did not embrace the organization's longstanding mission. Rather than continue Interlochen as an education center for the young, he "wanted to turn Interlochen into a Tanglewood, a professional place," an Interlochen trustee now recalls.

Nor did the new president have much feel for the other traditions that pervade Interlochen's surroundings. At the camp, for example, all the boys wear blue corduroys, the girls blue knickers. Shirts are powder-blue. The color of a camper's socks signals which division he or she is in. Even staff wear traditional blues. But the new president refused. "There was a core group who adhered to the old ways, and for them, the new appointee was moving too quickly and his behavior came off as insensitive," explains a trustee who was present during this stressful transition.

Board members quickly balked at the new president's vision, and his tenure lasted less than two years. But with his departure followed another period of caretaker management. Still at sea, board members decided to seek out a candidate more familiar with Interlochen's traditions. They turned to Roger Jacobi, a former staffer at the music camp who had gone on to become a prominent music educator. The board felt "Jacobi would be safe," says a trustee familiar with that period, and he was hired in 1971.

Although the decision turned out to be excellent, the selection of Jacobi was hardly systematic, reflecting Interlochen's disarray. As one trustee put it: "Even after the mistake that had been made [in hiring Jacobi's predecessor], there was never a series of formal interviews of Jacobi. At a 1971 board meeting, three candidates were interviewed, Jacobi being one of them. While at a concert he was attending, he was asked to take the presidency."

The Jacobi Years

"I am not the fire and brimstone type," says Jacobi with characteristic humility. "My style is quiet and pragmatic." After the colorful, blustery Maddy, Interlochen desperately needed a peacemaker who would pay attention to the most minute details. Jacobi did exactly that.

Jacobi had developed a fine reputation as a music educator and administrator with the Ann Arbor public schools and the University of Michigan. But for him, the position at Interlochen had its risks. First, there was the problem of walking in the shadow of a legend. "For years, people expected Joe to walk out of the woods like a mirage," Jacobi says. Even as Jacobi took over, Interlochen's financial situation was worsening.

Two challenges early in Jacobi's tenure helped him establish himself as a strong leader. The first involved a report on Interlochen's management and finances. The report, recalls Jacobi, "was approved by the board and put into a vault." Faculty who had provided input were furious. Jacobi made it a condition of his employment that the report be released. It was. He also took a strong stand over the firing of a faculty member who had been suspected of using marijuana. The dismissal, at the hands of an acting president who immediately preceded him, caused a great upheaval with the faculty. Jacobi arranged for full compensation for the aggrieved ex-employee, an agreement that resolved the matter for all concerned.

Such strong stands firmly established that Jacobi's administration would be guided by the principles of openness and fairness. Jacobi's next challenge was to stabilize Interlochen's finances. Maddy had gone on a building binge at Interlochen, authorizing construction throughout its 1,200 acres. When he did not get his way, the story goes, Maddy would dig the next hole himself. But the debt that resulted from Interlochen's overambitious capital activities was bleeding the budget. Jacobi stopped the feverish expansion. With assistance once again from benefactor Stone, Interlochen retired its long-term debt.

Jacobi next assembled a management structure. In addition to directors for the camp and the academy, Interlochen would have, for the first time, centralized finance, personnel, and public affairs functions, as well as a development office. Jacobi gave his administrators wide latitude to make decisions. Formal personnel policies were inaugurated. As Interlochen's management improved, enrollment in the camp and academy began to increase steadily, and the institution's operating budget was finally balanced.

Interlochen's board expanded during Jacobi's years, but by the mid-1980s, it still did not function very effectively. Because its membership is drawn nationally, with many members typically patrons of the arts, Interlochen's board faces special challenges. Integrating busy schedules and communicating over long distances are perennial problems. And though dedicated to Interlochen's mission, many members over the years have been unprepared to assume the governance, policymaking, and other responsibilities increasingly expected of nonprofit boards.

Stone served as board chair from the early 1970s until 1989, when, at the age of 87, he stepped aside and assumed the title of honorary chairman. Stone's passion for Interlochen is legendary, manifested by his years of service and unflinching willingness to donate funds. Yet, as a very busy executive slowed by advancing age, Stone could not be as fully involved in Interlochen's operations as its growing demands required. For much of Stone's tenure as board chair, Jacobi functioned as a "shadow chair," staff and board members now recall. The board, they say, was "dedicated but somewhat uninvolved." Jacobi set the stage for improvement.

In December 1987, Jacobi announced he would retire within three years. Thus alerted, the trustees asked him for one year's advance notice before he departed, and for criteria to guide the selection of a new president. The board was beginning to assume a more hands-on approach. In late 1988, Jacobi gave notice. Mindful of the earlier problems finding a successor to Maddy, the board "vowed to do a thorough job," one member recalls. A search committee was appointed. Jacobi advised the trustees to seek out a top administrator, not a glamorous name. He urged that prospective candidates respect the traditions of Interlochen. He suggested several possible successors. And he urged the new search committee to build a list of organizations and individuals to notify about the position opening.

Two thousand miles from Michigan, long-time Interlochen trustee Don Currie was home in Arizona when he learned the search committee had been activated. Currie, a former administrator with experience in personnel management, went to his typewriter and banged out a four-page letter to the chair of the nominating committee, brimming with ideas. Currie was asked to chair the search effort.

Currie's first task was to orchestrate a selection process. This became a subject of intense debate among board members. Several trustees argued vigorously for hiring an executive search firm. Others resolutely opposed the idea. "This time we wanted to do it the right way," a board member recalls. The board eventually decided against an outside search firm. But there was also debate over the composition of the search committee itself. In academic circles, faculty and student representatives typically serve on such committees. Interlochen's trustees decided to limit participation to board members while remaining open to all suggestions from alumni, faculty, and donors.

Currie handled his responsibility like a full-time job, engaging secretarial support from outside the institution. A generous trustee offered funds to pay for administrative needs such as printing, postage, and travel.

The search committee prepared a brochure outlining the responsibilities of the president's job and qualifications desired in a prospective candidate. Thousands of copies were distributed nationwide to alumni, arts groups, and other organizations. About seventy candidates made an initial cut, from which the search committee selected twelve. Each was interviewed intensively by at least two board members. The full search committee questioned the six finalists. "The process really worked," says Don Gonzales, an Interlochen trustee for more than fifteen years. In December 1989, the board hired Dean Boal, a former senior executive at National Public Radio with a long list of prestigious academic and professional credits. Equally significant as its choice, the board's "can do" approach to finding Jacobi's successor energized its members.

A New President Takes Up the Baton

Boal immediately set to work developing an agenda. Among his priorities: revisiting Interlochen's mission, developing a strong financial system, and fund raising. Boal formed three management teams to focus on these priority areas. Each was given three months to articulate its objectives.

In March 1990, Boal gave board members a report outlining his vision for Interlochen in the 1990s. "The board scrutinized the document, adding a goal that talks about fostering opportunities for professional growth and renewal," he says. The board's active response demonstrated a desire to sustain the more involved policy-setting role that it had launched beginning with the search committee.

Meanwhile, Boal is overseeing the drafting of new job

descriptions to serve as the basis for contracts and performance evaluations. He has introduced new computer technology at Interlochen and is changing the financial system. The staff, initially nervous about the transition to Boal, now welcomes the changes.

Interlochen, in Boal's view, is now moving into a "corporate era." Today's performers, he notes, "must be more in tune with audiences nurtured on television, who don't like listening to tuning or waiting for scene changes." And Boal has begun talking about the legacy he wants to leave at Interlochen when he departs, which he predicts will be in about ten years. "The board should really be in charge, and the school should be on the cutting edge in the 1990s as we enter the twenty-first century."

Chapter Eleven

Northside Center
for Child Development:
Managing
Leadership Transitions

———————◆———————

"I hate mental health." Those words are etched in the memory of Kate Harris. A decade ago she uttered them to her mother, Dr. Mamie Clark, the founder of the Northside Center for Child Development. "Dr. Mamie," as she was affectionately known, was approaching retirement and wanted her daughter to join her at Northside, a mental health facility in Harlem. Though Harris's background as a social worker made her the perfect candidate, the timing just was not right. At least not then.

"The first part of my mother's professional life was spent researching the damaging effects of racism and segregation on the development of self-esteem," Harris explains today. Clark wrote her master's thesis on the development of self-image in black children. The thesis had far-reaching impacts. It led to the founding of Northside — where black children "would receive appropriate care," Harris says. And Clark's writing, together with the work of her husband, Dr. Kenneth Clark, served as the research basis for the historic 1954 *Brown* v. *Board of Education* decision in the U.S. Supreme Court, outlawing "separate but equal" education in the public schools.

At a recent presentation at Northside, Kenneth Clark reminisced about the founding: "Mamie asked me to write to her father, a medical doctor, for a little money. I don't know why she didn't ask him herself. Her father asked for more information — and then provided that helping hand." The Clarks then turned to a small interracial band of friends and colleagues for assistance. Soon they moved into a basement office in Harlem and formally established Northside. The year was 1946. Confirmation of the Clark's fundamental assertion — that traditional models of psychology were ill suited, even destructive, for the children of the urban ghetto — came shortly thereafter, as this chapter will illustrate.

Today, Northside's staff tops one hundred. It is a richly credentialed group, populated with educators and a full range of therapists — a psychiatrist, psychologists, social workers. The budget exceeds $3.5 million annually; about 75 percent flows from government and 10 percent from Medicaid reimbursements. The remaining monies come from fund-raising events, the Greater Fund of New York (the New York United Way), private foundations, and corporations.

In 1984, the legacy finally passed to the next generation when Kate Clark Harris took over at Northside, For nearly half a century, the Clarks have toiled to kindle hope in Harlem. Northside is a children's mental health organization, an exemplary nonprofit. But Northside is also a story about a family, a most extraordinary family.

Clarks at the Helm

In the beginning, frustrated parents streamed to Northside to have their children evaluated. They feared the New York City Board of Education was inappropriately placing their children in classes for the mentally retarded. The Clarks, both psychologists, administered a battery of tests. They quickly discovered a pattern of misdiagnoses. "Kids living in the ghetto are bound to show the stress of that setting," Harris explains, "but that wasn't taken into consideration then."

"Eighty percent of the kids had IQs over the statutory

limit," Kenneth Clark says, punching the air with his finger for emphasis. Harlem newspapers picked up the story. The Clarks had proved their point.

Northside's client load swelled. Soon Mamie Clark realized that the families coming to the center for clinical problems exhibited other difficulties, too. A remedial reading school was started for children who manifested behavioral problems too severe to be handled in the conventional school system. Later, it was to evolve into a special elementary school and still later a preschool. The plate grew even fuller as other needs such as housing surfaced. "By the 1970s, there were two main programs — clinical and education — and a third dimension, which was advocacy," Harris explains. "In a community that knew mostly negatives," her father adds, "this was an oasis of concern."

The early days at Northside were a memorable blend of challenges, excitement, and growth. There was the loyal board, largely friends of the Clarks. Mamie Clark was firmly in charge of Northside's dedicated small staff. Ongoing funding, however, was a problem.

Despite the lengthening list of professional credits, the Clarks found that running against the prevailing school of Freudian therapy had shut them off from funding. But, an angel was in the wings — Marion Rosenwald Ascoli, the daughter of Julius Rosenwald, one of the founders of Sears Roebuck. "Without Mrs. Ascoli there wouldn't be a Northside," Harris says emphatically. "There wasn't the public or private funding to sustain it otherwise."

With its vision firmly planted, with a welcoming community, strong leadership, and financial support, Northside was humming. By the 1960s, its financial base had increased significantly, thanks to generous government support. The center moved to larger offices and expanded the staff. But beneath the surface, problems began to take root. "Kenneth and Mamie were benevolent dictators," a long-time Northside observer said. "Having a board that was hand picked, consummately loyal, and complacent resulted in an absence of governance."

Cracks began to show in the mid-1970s. New York City's fiscal woes hurt Northside's funding base. Mamie Clark commissioned organizational studies in 1974 and in 1977 to get a better sense of how administrative efficiency could be increased and to assess the agency's overall effectiveness. Among the issues were the need for board reorganization, improved agendas, better board attendance, and planning for the eventual selection of a new executive director. Northside's board, however, responded very slowly.

The Transition

Mamie Clark retired in 1979. When her mother asked Harris to take over, she refused. "I spent my years assiduously planning *not* to work for Northside," Harris says. The board began a search. "My mother had a successor in mind, but a few members of the board had their own ideas," Harris recalls. In an unusual act of independence, the board prevailed. An orderly transition had not been planned. "The board didn't know what to look for in a new executive director," explains Livingston Francis, a Northside funder and Clark family friend. "The board failed to provide needed direction and support." The newly appointed executive had little management experience. "It would have been tough for anyone to fill Mamie's shoes, and the combination of lack of experience and support doomed the new executive," Francis reflected. Adding to the new director's woes was a deficit.

The staff was increasingly unhappy. "Some had been at Northside over thirty years and were used to functioning a certain way," Harris said. The long-time controller resigned, leaving the financial records in chaos. A host of programmatic, administrative, and financial difficulties worsened in the early 1980s. Two staff members, in an act of insubordination, wrote the board listing their grievances, which ranged from not getting salary raises to dissatisfaction with management. The board was compelled to act.

Livingston Francis, then with the Greater Fund of New York, was asked to facilitate a board retreat. Shortly before it happened, Mamie Clark died, in 1983. "I can still feel the emotional intensity of that board retreat," Francis recalls. It was convened at the Clark house. "The board was beyond adolescence, already into adulthood, and had the wherewithal to do something," Francis says. "But some members were fearful of being viewed as disloyal, others untutored or reluctant to assert their responsibilities."

The weakness in the organization actually began when the Clarks formed Northside, Francis explains. "They understandably looked to friends." The new board members were not always knowledgeable about or committed to the organization, Francis says, "but they were loyal to the Clarks." Funders, too, were supporting the Clarks, not the institution. The patchwork of funding streams stitched together by the Clarks, each carrying its own special requirements, had created a managerial mess.

After the retreat, Francis put on his funder's hat and gave Northside the resources for a comprehensive management study. The embattled executive director departed, and the board began searching for a replacement.

Harris, at the time, had been a firsthand witness to Northside's managerial unraveling. She was on the board. At one meeting, a longstanding member nominated her to be executive director. This time she accepted, with two conditions: She would be "acting" director for a four-month period only, and the board was to keep the search committee active.

Harris had spent years avoiding this appointment. But looking across the office toward her desk, she says, "I knew this was home from the minute I sat in that chair." Her career had taken her from program to management, culminating in a position as director of a minority program for medical school applicants. In 1983, Harris now recalls, "I was ready, both professionally and personally to run Northside."

All eyes were on Harris. Because of the family connection, one colleague suggests, funders gave Harris more leeway than they would have given another executive director, especially after Northside's tumultuous early 1980s. "Harris was a logical bridge between the old and the new," says Livingston Francis.

By all accounts, Harris has managed Northside well. She understands intimately the organization's history and mission.

And she has used the benefits of her parents' extraordinary
legacy, Francis notes, even while reducing the presence of her
father. She has shown self-determination and willingness to take
risks.

One top priority has been to gain control of Northside's
finances. Harris moved rapidly to computerize and improve visi-
tation records. The original controller was somewhat secretive,
she explains. "There weren't irregularities, we just didn't know
the system and it was archaic." Even with regular financial
reporting to the board, she notes, "more than one person on
staff has to understand how the bookkeeping is done."

Harris's boldest decision was to eliminate Northside's
special-education elementary school. The city was absorbing
many of the kids into special programs, and Northside was not
in the financial position to compete with the Board of Education, its only source of referrals. Enrollments dropped by 50 percent between 1982 and 1984. In its place, Harris launched a
new program: a preschool for youngsters, age two and a half
to seven, with language, behavioral, or developmental problems. The new Early Childhood Center is a day treatment program providing clinical and educational assistance.

Within Northside, several areas need work, Harris acknowledges. At the staff level, there remain some rough edges
between departments and some personnel. Recently a consultant was asked to work with staff to clarify roles. Evaluation,
admits Harris, is also weaker than preferred. "I even asked the
board to evaluate me. They were reluctant at first, but finally
did it," she recalls.

Program evaluation also needs work. The records maintenance and treatment planning procedures required by the
government are not enough, Harris says. A new research and
evaluation department is in the works. It will evaluate Northside's services, keep on top of emerging community needs, and
generate research proposals.

Funding for nonprofits is never guaranteed, and Northside is no exception. The center is heavily dependent on government support, a mix of grants and contracts. As a United Way
agency (receiving about $18,000 annually), Northside is pro-

scribed from launching a major corporate campaign. Modest support has come from private foundations, and special fund-raising events have supplemented the budget. But a sneeze from government can turn into pneumonia at Northside.

Harris clearly understands the situation. On her desk sits correspondence about new regulations that could threaten the funding base for the outpatient clinic. "I'll be going to coalition-building meetings so we can fight these pending changes," she says.

Northside has created a new deputy director position to enable Harris to devote more attention to working with the board, doing outreach, and fund raising. The position was filled by a Northside staffer with fourteen years' experience. Though not explicitly stated, it can be a means of grooming Harris's successor. "I don't plan to be here forever," she says.

Northside has also been moving from organizational housecleaning to such longer-term matters as board development and expanding its mission to work more intensively with families and outreach into Harlem.

The Clark dynasty at Northside may come to an end. But Harris's careful effort to stabilize the institutional structure helps ensure that the family's inspiration will live on long after her departure. One key will be the board's willingness to commit fully to its responsibilities. Members have heard the message, and some changes are already underway.

Building the Board

Getting a board to change its ways is hard. Founders typically assemble their most loyal supporters, people whose primary allegiance is to the leader, not necessarily the mission of the organization. And board members frequently are not trained in their responsibilities. Francis, who is now with the Associated Black Charities, believes the prime danger is parochialism. "In the case of family founders," he observes, "it's even tougher to let go, to give the board responsibility, to let it govern."

A 1985 management improvement report concluded that the basic structure of Northside's board was fine. The problems were in its operation. The board did not function as a true governing body. More than one hundred recommendations were offered. Another study, focusing on the board committees, was done in 1987.

For outgoing board chair Bruno Quinson, "lack of personal commitment" is the prime board problem. Many members are business executives with limited time available. "It's difficult to get people to write letters or make calls, and to get them to pay personal attention to knowing the programs," Quinson explains. Only a small group can always be counted on, he says.

A new committee has been working to map out Northside's direction for the next decade. At an initial meeting, the mission was rewritten to reflect changes in the organization's direction. Later, working papers were produced with top staff, and a retreat held. The board eventually approved a new "plan of operation." Recommendations call for expanding services, targeting more family participation, and creating a research and evaluation department, a development office, and a training institute.

Hiring Harris proved to be a pivotal point in Northside's development. The organization has grown stronger by clarifying staff roles, fixing financial management problems, engaging in a long-range planning process, revisiting its mission, and producing an operating plan.

Postscript

An era at Northside came to an end in 1990. Kate Harris gave notice that she was leaving for an unexpected opportunity in Hong Kong. The board organized rapidly to establish a search committee and hire an executive search firm. A transition team composed of three department heads ran the organization while the search was being conducted. Sharon Foster-Johnson, then the executive director of the Girl Scouts of Greater New York, received an inquiry from the search firm. "I was sent the organization plan, it was marvelous, and I was hooked," says

Foster-Johnson. After a lengthy series of interviews with almost every board member and with senior staff, Foster-Johnson was offered the job.

One of her first activities during the first two months on the job was to meet with each of the one hundred staff members. She also established four immediate priorities for herself: (1) ensuring that the organization plan is a living document, and that staff members are informed and committed to its objectives; (2) making sure that accounting and personnel systems are operating smoothly; (3) looking at fund-raising opportunities; and (4) identifying research projects that would provide better information on the impact of Northside's programs.

Chapter Twelve

San Francisco Education Fund: A Pioneer Manages the Problems of Success

When San Francisco teacher Robert Valverde talks about "flour power," he's not leading a class on kneading dough. Valverde's is a modern message — to get teenagers to understand that having babies means big responsibilities. Donning surgical garb, he delivers "babies" — five-pound sacks of flour — to his teenage charges. Baby must go to classes or out on dates with the mother unless a babysitter is found. The rules are strictly enforced, and Valverde's pupils learn quickly that failing is a real possibility.

Valverde is one of over 1,000 teachers who have received grants of up to $1,000 per semester from the San Francisco Education Fund (SFEF). Founded in 1979, SFEF is one of the oldest of a growing group of local education funds across the country and a pioneer in many programs and fund-raising techniques.

Like many nonprofits, SFEF started with an abundance of good will and enthusiasm, and was quickly tempered by the harsh realities of raising money to survive. It faced a tough adjustment period in 1985 when the founding members of its dynamic board completed their terms and departed. Yet today,

94

SFEF aptly reflects the hallmarks of an excellent nonprofit. Its mission is clear and focused: to help the public school children of San Francisco by rewarding the creativity and motivation of good teachers. Its executive director is single-minded and devoted to the mission. Its board shares the same convictions; members are knowledgeable, experienced with nonprofits, and unrelenting in their search for financial assistance. SFEF's fundraising efforts include some of the most imaginative anywhere.

A New Organization Is Born

The original names on the letterhead brought instant recognition. The eight founders of the San Francisco Education Fund collectively had hundreds of years of experience serving on the boards of nonprofit organizations. They understood their roles, had a passion for the SFEF mission, and were primed to roll up their sleeves and work very hard.

Ruth Chance, former director of the Rosenberg Foundation and one of SFEF's founders, remembers those early days well. "There was building dissatisfaction in the schools. Proposition 13 and other rulings translated into declining resources. Timing was of the essence," she says. Joining Chance in forming SFEF was Leslie Luttgens, a former chair of the Council on Foundations. Both had lots of ideas about the school system, having recently finished work on a blue-ribbon education commission. The Cowell Foundation, which had been looking for a way to have an impact on schools, was anxious to help. Meetings were arranged with the superintendent. Eventually the notion of a fund that would give small grants to support teachers was born. The concept was not totally new. In nearby Oakland, the Marcus Foster Institute was already engaged in such activities.

The new entity that Luttgens and Chance set about to create would be different from most nonprofits. For one thing, it would serve a public institution — the school system. And it would distribute grants.

Often board members of new nonprofits are passionate about a mission, but have had little or no experience serving on a board. Composing bylaws, framing a committee structure, or determining terms of office are unfamiliar concepts. Early enthusiasm can easily turn into frustration in the face of the reality of trying to raise funds. Learning to separate policy setting from program development and management can be even more souring; new boards are frequently brimming with people excited about programs, not policies. SFEF's founders avoided these pitfalls. With an initial commitment of $50,000 from the Cowell Foundation, they paid a lawyer to draft bylaws, arranged for United Way to serve as a fiscal agent, and hired an executive director, Gladys Thacher.

"In the beginning it was me, an assistant, and a ficus tree," says Thacher, who remains SFEF's executive director today. Thacher was well known by SFEF's founders. She had already created a referral and counseling program to help teenagers learn about the workplace and a job counseling service for college-educated women. And Thacher knew about the schools.

By 1980, SFEF had a mission, an executive director, and a dynamic founding board—but no money to give grants. A founding board member stepped up and made a personal donation. Thacher personally turned to friends to raise more. She hired a grant writer. Gradually, funds started to come in. By 1982, SFEF was doing a lot more than simply giving out small grants to teachers. It began funding a "peer resources" program, where students help fellow students with problems; eventually, it spread from one pilot school to twenty-one. SFEF was fast becoming a "broker" between the schools and the broader community.

Telephone calls began coming in from California and around the country, people wanting to know about the SFEF model. The Ford Foundation asked SFEF to host a national conference. The meeting would help the foundation determine whether to fund local education funds in cities throughout the nation. For SFEF, the request promised to be a springboard for greater local and even national recognition. But it would require an enormous commitment. "Board members were conflicted," Thacher reports. "It was worrisome, yet the promise of bigger things ahead and more open doors was too good to reject."

The conference was a resounding success. SFEF's credibility increased dramatically. The Cowell Foundation renewed its funding. SFEF became a beehive of activity. Its relationship with the Ford Foundation spawned a new initiative: the San Francisco Math Collaborative, promoting collaboration among teachers and mathematicians from high schools, colleges, and private industry.

The Mission is Challenged

But with the spiraling growth came problems. SFEF's board had grown from the initial handful of founders to a larger and less seasoned group of over twenty. In 1985, after serving two consecutive three-year terms, most of the founders departed. "You must get off and let new people in," Luttgens says. "A board must refresh itself."

The transition was painful. "Starting small helped us establish strong bonds. Everyone had to work as a team," says current board president Harvey Schwartz. "Then we lost the anchors, the history, in one year."

There were other strains. Increasingly, generous donors came to SFEF offering funding for projects that fit their own priorities. SFEF undertook two new collaboratives similar to its math program with Ford: a science collaborative with the Carnegie Foundation and a humanities collaborative with the Rockefeller Foundation. At the staff level, day-to-day decisions also began leading the organization into new program areas. The group's mission was starting to get muddled. "People came to us with lots of ideas," Thacher explains. "When the really big foundations took an interest, we felt it could only help."

Internal board debate ensued. Should SFEF's mission continue to be its small grants program, or should it work to promote larger institutional change in the public school system? What should be done about initiatives generated by funders and SFEF's staff? "At times the board felt funders were dictating priorities," says one member. "At other times, we felt that the staff was charging ahead without board approval." SFEF's "family" ambience diminished. Delineating board roles and responsibilities became a pressing priority.

Meanwhile, school system officials had their own ideas about SFEF's role. For the fund to survive, cordial relationships with the school system were imperative. Getting itself into the position of instigating change on its own, or serving as the instrument of others, could have "turned the marriage into discord," says current superintendent Ramon Cortines. "There were times that I criticized SFEF and even refused to attend a press conference, because we weren't kept informed," he says. "I'm not concerned about the SFEF being involved in systemic matters, but if [it is], it must be with our full participation."

The debate over the mission redounded to staff members, who became increasingly anxious over their future in the organization. Accustomed to attending board meetings, some staffers got worried when the board went into executive session. Pulling back on new programs would mean clipping the staff's wings.

"I know that the board wasn't as clear as it needed to be about the activities we were undertaking," Thacher now says. Looking back, she notes, "The founders were so involved that details would have been redundant, but the new people needed more, and I didn't change my patterns as swiftly as needed to accommodate that." Eventually the board reasserted its dominance. Other programs were deemed important to SFEF's overall mission, but the small grants to teachers was to remain its centerpiece. Relations with the school board were clarified, and are now flourishing.

The board also made operational changes. It appointed strong committee chairs, identified gaps in board representation, and developed a board self-assessment process. It approved a staff organizational chart and formal job descriptions. The board authorized its strategic planning committee to review SFEF's mission statement. And it made plans for a retreat. By 1989, Thacher reports, "staff was more aware of the need for the board to meet in executive session, to exercise leadership and set overall policy."

As with most of SFEF's activities, the recasting of the board-staff relationship was undertaken with considerable thought. It has been painful for staff in the short run, but the changes have greatly strengthened SFEF as an organization.

Resource Development on a Roll

SFEF uses a range of diverse fund-raising strategies. Its long-standing relationship with the Cowell Foundation has been enviable. From the very beginning, Cowell provided operating support—a multiyear grant to pay for staff. This is a relatively unusual practice in the foundation world, where most funders prefer to support particular programs. SFEF was a new organization when Cowell began such funding, underscoring the grantmaker's uncommon willingness to take a risk. Clearly the expertise among SFEF's founding board was a prime factor.

Generating unrestricted monies remains an SFEF priority. The fund sponsors an annual holiday luncheon, has organized a permanent fund, and has generated an impressive list of individual givers. Collectively, these raise more than $300,000 annually that can be used for operating support.

The luncheon was the brainchild of SFEF executive director Thacher, who hit upon the idea of inviting corporations and other constituencies to an annual event celebrating the public schools. With an initial grant of $3,500, she hired a public relations firm to help with the first luncheon. That initial event attracted four hundred people and netted over $30,000. By 1989, attendance had swelled to over one thousand. And while the fee for the public relations firm has more than doubled, the net has quadrupled—to almost $120,000.

Having a luncheon as a major fund-raising event might seem a bit unusual. But the advantage, Thacher says, is that it attracts people during the day and asks them to commit only a couple of hours. The luncheon is held in December, when the spirit of giving already is high. The menu of hamburgers and fruit cups is supposed to be reminiscent of a school cafeteria. Colorful banners dress each table, which are also decorated with teddy bears with signs saying "Buy me." Each sale turns more revenue back to SFEF. Entertainment features student bands and singers. Students talk about what they learned from a SFEF teacher grantee. A few years ago, SFEF gathered famous graduates from the San Francisco public schools for an alumni chorus. San Francisco's mayor and school superintendent regularly attend.

A corporate chief executive officer is invited each year to host the event. He or she in turn is asked to identify two corporate cochairs, a classic fund raisers' pyramid strategy. The chair and cochairs are asked to write letters to other corporations seeking high-level support. Every year, a number of large corporations donate $3,000 to $5,000 each to sponsor whole tables. Individual tickets sell for $65. One of the most creative strategies is the "no-host" table. Thacher recognized that people like to come to events where they know others. And so each year, about forty people (typically including SFEF board members) are invited to be "no-host" organizers. Their job is to organize one table of ten friends and colleagues. Planning the entire event takes nearly a full year.

Building an Endowment

By 1985, SFEF development director Andrew Bundy explains "conversations began in earnest about getting a year ahead. We first thought of creating a reserve fund that we could dip into in bad times and set aside when things were okay." A reserve fund would permit SFEF to commit to a certain funding level for its small grants program for teachers, even if the exact level of funds that SFEF would raise that year was uncertain. Soon, the idea blossomed into the notion of creating a full-fledged SFEF endowment. The Cowell Foundation agreed to kick the drive off with a $250,000 grant. It also pledged an additional commitment of $500,000, on a one-for-three matching basis. (For every $3 SFEF raised, Cowell would kick in $1.) The endowment goal was ambitious: $3.3 million. "There was an element of innocence and hubris thinking it would be easy after getting the gift and challenge from Cowell," Bundy says.

To help with the drive, SFEF hired professional fundraising counsel. A feasibility study confirmed a broad base of potential supporters. A special "permanent fund" committee was established, cochaired by San Francisco Mayor Dianne Feinstein and Neil Harlan, retiring chief executive of McKesson Corporation. The committee recruited other prominent citizens to help. Two staff were hired to handle the administrative tasks.

LINCOLN CHRISTIAN COLLEGE AND SEMINARY

The permanent-fund committee divided into subcommittees on corporations, foundations, and individuals. Once a case statement was prepared, the drive was launched. Importantly, each donor was asked to permit some of his or her funds to be used to cover the campaign's operating expenses.

By early 1989, SFEF had raised $3 million. The Ford Foundation then awarded the group $300,000, enabling SFEF to reach its $3.3 million goal slightly ahead of its three-year projection.

Looking to the 1990s

"It is clear that the scenario has changed since 1979, when SFEF was the only kid on the block fund raising for the schools and acting as an intermediary," noted Thacher in her June 1989 report to her board. Challenges in the years ahead, Thacher wrote, include strengthening the board and management and making SFEF's funding self-renewing. She also wants to build alliances with other groups pursuing similar goals, to get more involved in early childhood education, cultivate more volunteers, and reach out into the broader community with efforts that appeal to families and children.

"Years ago we were in the wilderness, yelling about the need to champion the schools," says Thacher. A decade later, SFEF has made itself an exemplary nonprofit, knitting together the many threads of its community — from citizens to businesses to foundations to public officials — in a model effort to improve public education.

Postscript

Thacher retired in June 1990. A professional search firm was commissioned to recruit a new executive director, and Susan C. Wilkes succeeded Thacher in September 1990.

Chapter Thirteen

Seattle
Emergency Housing, Inc.:
Building Partnerships

Seattle is often described as chic, a city that overflows with trendy restaurants and an affluent younger set dressed in the latest gear from Eddie Bauer. But Seattle also has its other side — four thousand homeless people. During the 1980s, the affordable-housing crisis now affecting many parts of the United States struck this beautiful corner of the Northwest. Today, half of Seattle's homeless are families, mostly headed by single women. Children under the age of seventeen make up about two-thirds of the people in Seattle family shelters.

The Seattle Emergency Housing Service (SEHS) has been serving the city's homeless families since 1972. Back then, the homeless were mostly alcoholics and a few "bag ladies." The "deinstitutionalized mentally ill" were just beginning to trickle into the streets. Bob Sorenson and Sharie Todd founded the Seattle Emergency Housing Service using four housing units donated by a professor friend. It was the first facility for homeless families in the state, and one of the earliest in the nation. In those days, SEHS offered a short-term crisis service, providing shelter for two to four weeks. At the time, it seemed a straight-forward, focused, and limited caretaking role.

But times changed. By 1988, homeless families were streaming to SEHS facilities. It was able to help 295, but 2,183 families had to be turned away for lack of space. Nor was housing their only need. Most homeless families confront a constellation of difficulties, from poor educational achievement to health problems to periodic drug and alcohol abuse. Against such a backdrop, how can a nonprofit define a realistic mission and raise sufficient resources to carry it out? And how can it stimulate, refresh, and motivate its staff and board in an environment that could be consumed with hopelessness?

SEHS has addressed these questions with uncommon success. Its mission—"serving homeless families"—remains paramount. Its leadership is creative and bold. Its board, activist and dynamic, is one of the finest anywhere. And the public-private partnership that SEHS has knitted together to finance its program stands as a national model.

Seattle Fosters Partnership

"Seattle is not a turf-oriented city," says Martha Dilts, who has been SEHS executive director since 1976. "There's a habit of coalition building here." That local culture enabled SEHS to stabilize early and grow in response to needs. In 1972, as their efforts were just getting underway, Sorenson and Todd shipped off a funding request for about $300 to the local Medina Foundation. Little did the two founders realize that they were about to find an angel in the foundation's Greg Barlow. "The modest size of the request caught the foundation's attention," says Dilts. "A subsequent site visit resulted in the start of what evolved into an enduring relationship."

In 1975, Barlow introduced SEHS to the King County United Way. Having already identified homelessness as a growing problem, United Way required little convincing about the need. But it wondered if a more experienced organization or agency would be better to handle the problem of homeless families. None could be found. So United Way agreed to a special "contract for services" with SEHS. That would defray some operating expenses of two staff — an executive director and assistant — and help pay the rent. By 1978, SEHS became a United Way member agency, stabilizing SEHS's operating support and, equally important, signaling to other funders that SEHS was worthy of support.

Even as United Way was coming aboard, SEHS caught the attention of the Seattle Housing Authority (SHA), the city's public housing agency. SHA agreed to provide ten units of emergency housing to SEHS to shelter its families for up to four weeks. Such an arrangement between a public housing agency and a nonprofit was highly unusual in 1975. Five years later, the housing authority delivered another twenty-one units to SEHS for "transitional housing," where families could stay for up to six months and receive comprehensive social services. The city, meanwhile, began channeling federal Community Development Block Grant monies to help SEHS defray its operating costs. The housing authority also offered office space. In May 1989, SEHS moved into newly remodeled quarters in a public housing complex with thirty-one emergency housing units, a resident manager's apartment, office space, a food bank, and a child-care center.

A Working Board

SEHS's board has achieved a performance level sought by many nonprofit boards but achieved by few. Both former and current board presidents insist there are "no tricks and no magic — just people willing to work hard to achieve the mission."

Board meetings are monthly, committee work requires additional time, and special events add to a board member's busy agenda. Nevertheless, attendance is routinely over 60 percent. Special events, such as retreats and fund raisers, will get nearly 100 percent participation. SEHS's sparse bylaws set no upper limit on the number of board members and identify no board committees. There is no length or limit on terms. Typically the SEHS board has fifteen to twenty members.

Reminders of the organization's humble beginnings are still evident sixteen years after its founding. SEHS board members are not among Seattle's bluebloods. Rather, they are city and county officials, middle managers from area companies, and a handful of professionals. Many have had little experience with nonprofit organizations. "We're looking for real commitment — not necessarily political or financial clout," explains Amy Laly, current board president. Formerly a budget analyst at United Way, where she reviewed SEHS's financial statements, Laly asked to join the board. Other members, like former president John Braden, were recruited. A city employee, Braden filled SEHS's need for financial expertise and knowledge about public funding.

"From the beginning," Dilts noted, "we were blessed with hardworking volunteers who understood the role of a board member. The nominating committee isn't looking for people with the same skills as staff." (The SEHS staff is mainly social service professionals.) When SEHS added a new housing initiative that required an understanding of development, the organization recruited a contractor and architect to its board. SEHS board orientation efforts are especially noteworthy. Prospective board members first meet with a current member, often over lunch to get briefed on the organization. They next meet other staffers, and finally, attend a formal board meeting. New members are invited aboard as needs dictate.

When Laly took over as board president in 1989, she set about immediately to build a strong partnership with SEHS executive director, Martha Dilts. A longstanding board member, Laly had known Dilts for a decade. Yet both set aside special time to discuss communications, agenda development, and other issues vital to the smooth functioning of the organization. In fact, this same operating procedure is carried out with every new board president. "The president/executive director relationship is the key relationship in the organization," Dilts explains.

There's little in the basic structure or process at SEHS that seems different from other organizations. Probe deeper, however, and the sense of bonding and commitment of its board members stands out. First, there's the board philosophy. As Laly puts it: "We're not elitist, we want all to participate. We battle over ideas and keep that separate from the individual."

Both Laly and Braden found that the experience of presiding over the board offered personal and professional rewards. Says Braden: "I really didn't know how to run a meeting, when to bring closure, how to be a quick study, or know to get people enough information. Becoming board president nurtured those skills." Braden believes a board president's job calls for the following qualities and skills: commitment, even passion, for mission; good communication and interpersonal skills; an ability to involve people in making decisions; the capacity to learn quickly and to bring issues to closure; supervisory experience; and a commitment to working in partnership with staff.

Several SEHS board practices contribute to its effectiveness. For example, agenda for board meetings are developed with the executive director and reviewed by the SEHS executive committee beforehand. Board meetings run about two hours, once a month. Punctuality is encouraged: At one time a board rule stipulated that members who came five minutes late paid $5. Though the penalty was never invoked, its message was heard. Absent board members telephoned. Members who cannot fulfill their obligations are asked to resign. All board members pledge a gift. The SEHS executive director attends board meetings. Other staff are not excluded, but it is understood that the executive director represents their interests.

Each year, SEHS sponsors two half-day board retreats, typically scheduled on Saturday mornings. One is used to discuss fund raising and to plan for SEHS's annual phonathon; the other examines planning and other business. An annual board/staff retreat is also held.

Fund Raisers

Though the city of Seattle and United Way still provide about 80 percent of its budget, SEHS has pressed hard to diversify its funding base. Contributions from individuals, corporations, and foundations have all increased in the past five years. One of the most unusual fund-raising events is the annual dinner and dance sponsored by the "Post-Holiday Soirée Fund-Raising Council."

The council is a group of well-connected young professionals who wanted to turn their party-planning skills into an activity that would benefit others. Launched in 1986 by four young men who had honed their hosting skills at college bashes, the group decided to focus on one issue — helping homeless families. A telephone call to United Way led them to SEHS. Three soirées later, the group has expanded to a working committee of about ten. Each year, the event has grown in participants and funds raised. Held a few weeks after Christmas, the 1989 soirée netted SEHS almost $23,000.

Members of the soirée working committee work closely with Dilts and her development officer, planning even the most minute details. Graphic and printing services are donated. The soirée's young sponsors do not end their involvement when the party is over. Several are now involved on the SEHS board, others have donated technical expertise and a computer, and they are busy planning next year's event.

The other main fund raiser is the annual phonathon, which raises over $18,000 a year. Phones and space are donated by local corporations. The event is held over two nights, from 7:00 to 9:00. The average donation has jumped from less than $25 to over $45. About one in five gifts exceeds $100. SEHS projects earnings from the phonathon will rise to $30,000 by 1991, since the group has computerized its donors lists and hired a full-time development director.

Orchestrated primarily as a fund-raising strategy, the phonathon has also turned out to be a superb board development tool. All board members are expected to participate. Each is asked to identify friends who might give. Since many have never solicited funds, which can be uncomfortable, each member receives a short course from SEHS's fund-raising consultant. Before hitting the phones, board members get a script, lists, and guidelines. A prepared statement describes SEHS's mission, and tells exactly how far the prospective donor's gift will go toward providing shelter for a homeless family. Board alumni join current members for the phonathon.

What's in the Future?

SEHS has achieved an unusually good balance between a strong executive director and strong board. Dilts is very humble, but a big part of the success of SEHS is due to her vision, tenacity, persistence, and team-building skills. She is caring and compassionate, but also very task oriented. Trained as a professional social worker, Dilts had just returned from an Alaskan sojourn when she applied for and got the job as SEHS executive director thirteen years ago. Today, she is a nationally recognized speaker and innovator.

What would happen to SEHS if Dilts left? "We're savvy to her skills, the staff know their jobs, the board is strong and all the essential systems — financial, personnel, management — are in place," says former board chair Braden. Dilts delegates a good deal of responsibility to her staff. Staff members play a key role in hiring decisions, are encouraged to be creative with their programs, and are asked to build relationships with other organizations. Such outreach yields numerous rewards, including staff satisfaction and innovative programs. Staff members are kept fresh and informed of changes that might affect their efforts. At a program level, outreach has led to cooperative agreements with local agencies to provide health care, child care, and employment referrals.

These activities keep people challenged, which is one reason why in an environment that could easily lead to burnout, staff stay at SEHS for many years. Dilts has no immediate plans to leave. She feels much work remains, since the problem of homelessness is not diminishing. Though no one is explicitly being groomed for her position, the infrastructure of SEHS is so solid that the question of leadership succession is unlikely to be a problem.

Chapter Fourteen

Upward Fund Afterschool: Leadership for Independence

On December 11, 1988, "Gorby fever" was peaking as midtown Manhattan prepared for a visit from the Soviet leader. About three miles uptown, Harlem was experiencing a special visit of another sort: Wayne Gretzky and the Los Angeles Kings. "Hockey isn't usually thought of as a sport for minority kids," says Gene Kitt. "But that's exactly why we wanted to bring a professional team here."

Kitt is the executive director of Upward Fund Afterschool, a late-afternoon haven for kids from some of the meanest streets of the world. Children in the Upward Fund programs are introduced to new ideas: from hockey or fishing to computer training, field trips, or visits from professional Hispanic and Afro-American women. Upward Fund makes children feel special and keeps them from being sucked into the drug contagion of Harlem.

Sports are a central part of the program, but education is the glue. The Kings' visit was the launching pad for Upward Fund starting Harlem's first hockey school. What does this have

109

to do with education? "Hockey is played in over twenty cities," Kitt explains. "We start by asking students to locate Edmonton."

Upward Fund was created in 1977. Back then it focused on teenagers with dreams of becoming basketball stars. "The superstar model dominated," Kitt explains. "We had to shift the aspirations and get kids to learn the importance of education. Our kids needed work skills, not ball-playing skills."

In 1981, Upward Fund launched its first educational venture, a summer computer camp. Kitt worked out a deal to borrow twenty computers from a local program called "Play to Win." Soon more than one hundred kids were typing away at the keyboards. A fund raiser generated $20,000, enabling Upward Fund to buy computers of its own. Summer enthusiasm spilled over into the school year. By 1982, Kitt reflects, "we had over eight hundred kids and it was turning into chaos."

Over the next five years, Upward Fund expanded its education programs and established its roots. By 1986, confident in its programs, the organization began building its institutional capacities and financial framework. Today, there is a wealth of offerings for underprivileged kids aged six to nineteen in East and Central Harlem. Parents can attend a new adult literacy course while their children choose from a rich variety of programs, ranging from homework tutorials to computer literacy to workforce preparation. There are excursions, too, from fishing trips to museum visits. At its start, Upward Fund had fewer than 50 participants; today, it serves more than 1,200 each year. The annual budget averages about $500,000, nearly all from private sources.

Upward Fund can credit much of its success to the personal commitment of Edgar Bronfman, chairman of the board and chief executive officer of the Seagram Company. Most nonprofit organizations start with a grassroots board and then dream up special advisory mechanisms to attract corporate participation. At the Upward Fund, it happened in reverse. Over the years, Seagram has provided a wide range of assistance, from dollars ($137,000 in 1987) to board members, office space to technical expertise. Blending the ample skills and capacities of this corporate giant with the vision and street smarts of the program staff has made for a powerful union.

Support from Seagram

In 1980, as Upward Fund's afterschool athletic program began to swell, the group sought a building of its own. Ned Foss, then Seagram's special programs consultant, was dispatched to help arrange for the fund to acquire a property in East Harlem and convert it to a gym. Foss soon became the fund's executive director. After the new building was purchased, it turned out to be unsuitable. But it had appreciated and the $800,000 it brought at sale was invested, with the interest used to defray Upward Fund's operating costs. Seagram's business manager, Frank Raysor, manages the investment fund. He also serves as Upward Fund's treasurer.

Seagram also sponsors an annual "harvest tasting" to raise money for Upward Fund, turning out affluent New Yorkers for a festive sampling of the industry's products. Seagram uses its own ample network and takes care of all the details from invitations to protocol. Typically the event raises about $100,000.

By 1986, Seagram felt it was time to review Upward Fund's accomplishments and determine where the organization should be headed. Ned Foss was departing as Upward Fund's executive director, and Kitt, who was then program director, was moving up to take over administrative responsibilities. Seagram wanted the fund to become more financially independent. "We want self-sufficiency for Upward Fund, but realistically it's very tough," says Dan Paladino, a Seagram vice president and an Upward Fund officer. The time for nudging the fund toward independence had arrived.

An organizational assessment was commissioned to figure out how best to get Upward Fund up on its own two feet. The primary recommendation: Upward Fund should pursue a diversified fund-raising strategy, including special events and outreach to individual and institutional support. The fund should determine what captivates prospective donors and develop a case statement. At the organizational level, Upward Fund should hire its own development staff and expand its board to diminish Seagram's role. In response, Upward Fund hired a fund raiser and set in motion plans to increase its board to fourteen, with more local community representation.

The strategic plan to put the fund on sound financial footing calls for tapping more corporate and foundation donors and developing new fund-raising events. It recommends reviewing the fee structure for Upward Fund's programs, especially the summer camp. For the board, the plan recommends a pledge policy for each board member. "I'd like to buy a building," adds Kitt. "We now pay over $25,000 yearly in rent to the Board of Education."

Today, the pressure to raise its own funds intensifies as Seagram's financial support gradually diminishes. The company is also trying to decide whether to continue the harvest tasting event and to keep providing office space for Upward Fund. Kitt is not afraid to cut the umbilical cord. "The relationship to Seagram has had strong pros and cons," he says. "Because [Seagram is] so well known and well endowed, other funders seem to assume that we could always go to the well for more. On our financial statement, the proceeds from the building sale—which we really can't tap—look like our pockets are bulging."

Already, Upward Fund is making progress. Its list of private donors is growing. Board members have taken on responsibility for major fund-raising events, including a concert at Lincoln Center organized by board members Willie Fry and Marvin Wilkinson. The New York Yacht Club recently hosted a sports auction for the fund, thanks to the efforts of advertising executive, sailing enthusiast, and new board member Martin Puris.

Board member Emily Gates from *Gourmet* magazine is also pitching in her talents. Her work on other nonprofit boards, including the Junior League and Henry Street Settlement, was not as fulfilling as Upward Fund, she says. "The fund gives me free rein, it's really grassroots, and the sky is the limit," she explains. Doing fund raising "requires a good cause, a product to sell, getting the message out, thinking about what people want to do, and pricing the ticket," she says. "I've been to the program and seen its impact. I wish my kid's day-care program knew as much about learning processes as Gene and his staff have figured out."

Discipline with Love

Gene Kitt travels every day to the crack-infested streets of East Harlem. From the discreet chirping of contemporary telephones and quiet tapping of computer keyboards to boom boxes blasting rap and reggae, Kitt lets nothing distract his focus from the kids. His philosophy: "Rich or poor, kids got to grow up in a love situation."

Kitt is a gifted leader. He is tough yet warm. And he loves kids. Youngsters who may be recalcitrant during the schoolday are clay in Kitt's hands. He is a storyteller. Through his stories and his actions, his leadership and management styles emerge. Kitt readily admits he is a "learner in management." But as one board member put it, this "manager in training" has a steep learning curve, especially for financial management and budget development. To supplement on-the-job training, Kitt is pursuing a master's degree in nonprofit management. For one assignment, he is preparing Upward Fund's first board manual. His motivation to improve does not go unnoticed. Says one staff member: "Mr. Kitt is always pushing us and the kids harder, but we see how hard he pushes himself."

Listening to Kitt, one learns the principles that guide him: Ensuring safety. Maximizing parent involvement. Providing structure and clear rules consistently enforced. In short, "discipline with love." Kitt's operating tenets include listening to all sides, good manners, respect, and neutrality. "It's not how you start," he says, "but how you finish." As for his staff, Kitt says: "I want them to care about the kids, but they know they are not to become surrogate anythings. Staff must leave their own needs and problems at the door. I want professionals here." These are common principles, the basis for good management. But Kitt brings "value added" through his own contagious enthusiasm and his standard as a role model who lives his principles.

Kitt is perpetually in motion. Even when he is sitting still, his mind is like a popcorn popper. Kitt has the capacity to take an idea, mold it, and make a sale. A prime example is the special program he launched in 1989 by taking advantage of two truisms: Kids love baseball. And corporate executives often get free tickets to baseball games.

The seed for the program was planted when board member Emily Gates introduced Kitt to Pete Hunsinger, a *Gourmet* magazine senior executive who loves both baseball and kids. Kitt asked him to take a youngster to a game as a special reward for improvement — either in school, at home, or with peers. Then the idea grew. "I realized this would be a great opportunity to ask an executive to serve as a mentor," Kitt explains. "It wouldn't demand much time, just take one kid, two or three times in a season. And we would take care of the transportation and supervision by having a staff member along."

Kitt asked Hunsinger to enlist executives from other firms to sign on as baseball mentors. More than twenty did. But Kitt had one more request. He asked the mentors to send a letter to their charges after the game, since his kids so seldom get any mail. "We make sure the kid sends a letter in return," Kitt adds. Even while Gates was being interviewed for this profile, Kitt was at it again. This time he found a *Gourmet* staffer who agreed to take the kids sailing.

Rule #1: Rules Cannot Be Broken

"We labor to create a safe and secure environment. This is a priority," Kitt asserts.

Glass litters the schoolyard near where Kitt stands as he explains Upward Fund's activities. Scanning the local landscape with his index finger, he points out the areas where crack cocaine is routinely sold. As kids file in to Kitt's afterschool program, a $60,000 BMW with gold hubcaps and opaqued windows sits brazenly at the school's front door. "It's a war zone in the streets," Kitt says. "When the kids come here we want it to be an oasis."

A staff member knows never to leave his charges alone.

Going on trips — to museums or parks or other outings — is part of the Upward Fund's enrichment strategy. But trips require coordination, transportation, and a lot of supervision. One day, a staffer left a child on a subway. Kitt promptly fired him. The aggrieved ex-staffer took his complaints to the community, enlisted several local political leaders in his cause, and succeeded in getting people so aroused that they decided to march against Kitt. Kitt convened a community meeting, complete with a Spanish translator, and heard the people's complaints. "Apparently [the fired staff member] failed to tell them that he had left a child alone," Kitt says. "I said to these parents, how would they feel if it was their child?" He got his point across.

After tensions died, one community leader asked Kitt to rehire the staffer. Kitt flatly refused. "Rules are there not to be broken, not to give mixed messages," he explains. "And nothing is more important than the kids' safety."

Even Little Rules Have Big Messages

Youngsters who participate in Upward Fund's programs are expected to pay a $3 fee. "It would never stand in the way of a kid participating," Kitt says, adding that the children "also get a card and must have a picture taken." Such seemingly trivial items, in the Kitt philosophy, are designed to subtly convey responsibility and draw in parental involvement.

Another Kitt maxim is respect for others. "Cooperation isn't normally important to these kids, so we take every opportunity to reinforce working together and getting them to think about others' feelings," he explains. With a twinkle, Kitt adds: "We even have a class in etiquette." Board member Gates underscores its value. She organized an event for teens to meet with female Afro-American and Hispanic professionals. "They were enthusiastic, interested — and cleaned up after the meeting!" she says.

Kitt launches into a story about a disgruntled and disrespectful youngster who became particularly nasty to his father. "I took the kid and his father into my office," Kitt says. "The kid was slouched with his hand holding up his head. So I asked the kid, 'Who gave you that hand?'" Finally, says Kitt, the child answered that his father had. Kitt did not let up. "I asked him, 'Who paid for those expensive sneakers?'" Getting the same response, Kitt then asked the boy to hold out his hand to his father. "This environment runs on respect, for the kids, among peers, with parents," Kitt says.

Building a Sound Organization

Executive directors who become an organization's best asset can also be its greatest liability. Could Upward Fund survive if Kitt should depart? Board members acknowledge they worry about this possibility. It would hurt, one said, but the organization has a clear program structure, product, and need. The staff know their jobs.

Upward Fund has an increasingly solid infrastructure. It likely could survive changes in board structure, in financial makeup, and, if need be, in its management.

PART THREE

ACHIEVING EXCELLENCE

In Part One we identified and described four hallmarks that distinguish the excellent nonprofit organization and cited evidence to support the importance of these factors. The case studies in Part Two illustrated the interaction of the characteristics of excellence over time in ten different organizations that had been identified as outstanding examples in their community.

We now turn to an examination of ways the staff and volunteer leadership of the typical nonprofit can apply the hallmarks and turn them into action steps. In each chapter we include a series of questions for self-analysis, to help readers apply general principles to their own unique situations. Throughout this section we selectively cite publications that will be useful to those who wish to explore a particular subject in greater depth.

Chapter Fifteen

Making Mission Meaningful: Building and Using a Strong Mission Statement

Nonprofit organizations are unique in that they have enormously wide latitude in which to operate. They must conduct their activities within the laws governing their incorporation and tax-exempt status, of course, but otherwise the strictures are few. The mission statement thus becomes the prime vehicle for defining the purpose and scope of the organization's activities. In short, it creates the standard and the overarching goal of the organization.

It might be helpful to view the mission statement as serving a function akin to the profit motive in the private business world. Just as all corporate officers know their ultimate goal is to make money for the company, nonprofits exist to achieve their mission. And that mission must be understood and accepted by everyone serving the nonprofit institution, from governing trustees to staff to volunteers.

The mission statement is the nonprofit's guidepost. It is the starting point for the development of plans and programs. It serves as a criterion for judging the appropriateness of new

119

activities or reevaluating longstanding ones. And it is a rally-ing point for commitment. For the nonprofit in search of excel-lence, there is no substitute for a clearly articulated, broadly understood mission statement.

Guidelines

A mission statement should succinctly describe what the organi-zation does, whom it serves, and what it intends to accomplish. It should:

- Be understandable to the general public.
- Be brief; not more than one or two sentences or a short para-graph.
- Be realistic in light of the organization's current and antici-pated financial and human resources.
- Be specific enough to provide the base for developing ob-jectives and programs that carry out the mission.
- Be broad enough to stand the test of time so that it need not be revised frequently.
- Be an accurate reflection of the governing board's intent and understanding of the organization.
- Be operational; state the expected outcome, not just declare good intentions.

The Importance of Process

For "true believers" anxious to launch an organization, the no-tion of process may sound dull. In fact, following the right process is crucial to developing a mission statement that is widely endorsed and can stand the test of time.

Well-established organizations typically develop and re-view their mission statements as part of a long-range strategic planning process. This ensures the maximum involvement of the senior staff and the board, which must ultimately give final approval. When key people in the organization are an integral part of the process, they are more likely to embrace the mission and communicate it to others.

The American Symphony Orchestra League, for example, asked the long-range planning committee of its board to develop a mission statement in 1986. A professional consultant assisted in the process. The exercise was enormously valuable, the League reports. "The concepts of leadership and service, the emphasis on the balance of artistic, organizational and financial strength of orchestras, and adding an 'external' component (communicating to the American public) provided the complete framework for the plan," League officials note. "The statement was endorsed by our members so there was agreement and 'buy-in' early on. The mission statement helps, too, as we evaluate suggestions for new programs that we receive from members, funders, or develop here on the staff."

In drafting mission statements, some nonprofits turn to their volunteer membership or local chapters for help. The American Cancer Society surveyed its fifty-seven constituent divisions when revising its mission statement. And Family Service America, which reviewed its mission as part of an extensive planning process, used market research to solicit the views of all its members, some 80 percent of whom responded.

Involving a lot of people in drafting a mission can be time consuming. It took eighteen months for a high-level board and officer committee to create a mission statement for InterAction, a coalition of international humanitarian groups. "Then it took another six months to have it fully discussed and finally adopted by the full board," the group reports. Ultimately, however, the mission is so vital to an organization's success that it is worth the time and effort to do it right.

Examples of Mission Statements

The following samples illustrate the mission statements of a wide range of nonprofit organizations:

The American Heart Association (AHA)

It is the mission of the American Heart Association to reduce disability and death from cardiovascular diseases and stroke.

Every word in the statement is important, explains Dudley Hafner, AHA's executive vice president. Slight but significant changes are made about once every four or five years. The most recent was to add the word "stroke" to the mission statement. The point, Hafner explains, was to call particular attention to the problems of stroke, even though that ailment is already included in the term "cardiovascular disease." The association also took out the word "premature" from before "disability and death" because, Hafner says, it is now scientifically verified that heart disease is not a function of aging.

Evangelical Council for Financial Accountability (ECGA)

The Council exists to increase the public's confidence in the business affairs of evangelical organizations by:

1. Establishing standards
2. Helping organizations meet the standards
3. Certifying compliance
4. Communicating with the public

In recent years, ECGA president Arthur Borden reports, his organization has focused especially on the mission's fourth objective, communicating with the public, to assure potential donors that contributions made to ECGA-certified groups will be properly used.

The Council of Jewish Federations

A few years ago, the council published an extensive set of guidelines to help local federations develop their own long-range plans. The process called for each federation to develop its own mission statement as the first step in the planning process. Here's how two local federations defined their mission:

The mission of the Toronto Jewish Congress is to serve as the central Jewish communal organization dedicated to the preservation and enrichment of Jewish life in the Greater Toronto area and to the perpetuation of the community's identification with Israel.

The mission of the Allied Jewish Federation of Denver is to sustain and protect our local community of Jews; to assure that the material, social, psychological, educational and spiritual needs of its members are adequately met; to fulfill its obligations toward Israel; and to inculcate the sense of Klal Yisroel so that each individual Jew feels responsible for the sustenance and survival of the local, the national, and the international community of Jews.

Citizens' Scholarship Foundation of America (CSFA)

CSFA developed a statement that defines its mission and succinctly spells out how it is to be carried out.

Citizens' Scholarship Foundation of America is a national, nonprofit student aid service organization. CSFA's mission is to expand access to higher education by involving and assisting the private sector in the support of students and in the encouragement of higher levels of educational achievement.

In carrying out its mission, CSFA plays a leadership role in providing high quality, innovative, personal, and efficient services to communities, companies, foundations, associations, and individuals.

INDEPENDENT SECTOR

To create a national forum capable of encouraging the giving, volunteering and not-for-profit initiative that help all of us to better serve people, communities and causes.

Formulated by the INDEPENDENT SECTOR organizing committee in 1979, this mission provides the basis for developing program goals and for each five-year plan. It appears in abbreviated form on the bottom of INDEPENDENT SECTOR stationery to continuously communicate the mission to board, staff, membership, and the general public.

The American Cancer Society (ACS)

This association conducted a national survey of its volunteers and staff to reexamine its mission and the working of its mission statement. Originally, the mission read:

> The American Cancer Society is a voluntary organization and exists to eliminate cancer as a human disease, to save more lives from cancer, and to diminish suffering from cancer through research, education and service.

Based on survey results and the work of an ad hoc committee, the mission was revised to read:

> The American Cancer Society is the nationwide voluntary health organization dedicated to eliminating cancer as a major health problem by preventing cancer, saving lives from cancer and diminishing suffering from cancer through research, education and service.

Why the changes? The society reports that the word "nationwide" was added to signify that the organization was both national and community-based and to differentiate ACS from similar organizations. Adding the word "health" was designed to further clarify the type of voluntary organization ACS is. The new mission keeps the strong visionary phrase "eliminating cancer" but qualifies it by adding "as a major health problem"—a goal that may be more possible. And ACS included "preventing cancer" in its new mission to highlight prevention as a major focus of its research and better reflect new public attitudes about the disease.

Using the Mission Statement

The excellent organization strives to keep its mission alive in the hearts and minds of volunteers, staff, and board. Successful nonprofits approach this challenge in a variety of ways; here are a few examples:

- The Evangelical Council for Financial Accountability expects all organizations applying for membership to provide a copy of their mission statements. Each year, it asks its member groups to send copies of any rewritten missions. The goal is to help each ECFA member become aware of the importance of a mission statement.
- The American Association of University Women prints its mission statement on all brochures and publications.
- The American Cancer society produces a poster-sized version of its mission statement for all its offices and affiliates. ACS also prints the statement on the reverse side of the national staff's business cards.

Revisiting the Mission

In an ideal world, all mission statements would stand the test of time. In the real world, changes are sometimes inevitable. Major changes in an organization's direction should always be reflected in the mission statement. To maintain its significance as the organization's basic guide, the mission must retain its currency and relevance at all times. When drafting or revising a mission statement, the nonprofit should insist on the same care and involvement used to write the original mission.

Good organizations revisit their mission statements regularly. Changes can often happen subtly and gradually, the cumulative result of day-to-day operating decisions. At a minimum, the mission should be reexamined whenever long-range plans are being reviewed or developed. That process is typically undertaken every three to five years in the best-managed nonprofit organizations.

Questions for Self-Analysis

- Does your mission statement fulfill the criteria listed earlier in this chapter?
- How satisfied are you with your mission statement and would you recommend any changes now?
- When was it last reviewed or revised and what process was followed?
- If you asked your board members at their next meeting to each write the organization's mission statement on a blank paper, what would be the result?
- How have you undertaken to communicate the mission to board, staff, volunteers, and members?

Chapter Sixteen

Developing
Leadership Skills

———————◆———————

Confronting the subject of leadership is perhaps the most daunting challenge of all. The presence of an effective leader is the
sine qua non of the truly excellent organization. But how does
one recognize a leader? How does the organization seeking to
hire a new executive director determine whether the prime candidate will be a leader? How can staff executives assess their
own talents and improve their leadership ability?

Fortunately, the subject of leadership has been studied
in depth, and there is broad agreement on several factors affecting the development of leaders:

- Leaders are not born; they are made.
- Certain skills that are helpful to leaders, such as effective
  oral and written communication, can be acquired through
  training.
- Workshops led by skilled trainers can sharpen people's perceptions of themselves and give insights into how they are
  perceived by others. But courses cannot teach essential lead-

127

ership characteristics such as vision, character, or maturity.
- Many leaders have, to use Warren Bennis's term, "invented
  themselves" through their own self-development.

Two recent books may be especially helpful to those interested in developing their leadership abilities: *On Leadership*
(Gardner, 1990) and *On Becoming a Leader* (Bennis, 1989a).

To help nonprofit groups better identify and develop their
leaders, we have synthesized the thinking of several authorities
in the field. We have also devised a series of questions that can
be used by leaders for self-study or by nonprofit boards assessing potential candidates for leadership positions.

We draw our portrait of the effective leader from the conclusions of the focus group of experienced consultants and nonprofit executives convened for this project, and from the writ-
ings of John Gardner, Warren Bennis, and Brian O'Connell
(see References section). From these, six fundamental characteristics of quality leadership emerge.

1. Presence of a guiding vision characterized by long-term
    thinking.
2. Ability to convey the vision to others, to motivate and ex-
    cite them.
3. Strong self-understanding, integrity, candor, and maturity.
4. Strength of convictions and toughness to stand by them.
5. Willingness to take risks, to be daring, and to learn from
    mistakes.
6. Ability to master the organization and its context, rather
    than surrendering to it.

A Guiding Vision

The effective leader takes a long-term view of his or her organization, looking beyond the latest crisis or the quarterly report.
This leader has a clear idea where the organization should go
and what it should be several years in the future. Vision is what
distinguishes the top-notch leader from the ordinary manager.

Or, as Bennis puts it: "The manager has his eye always on the bottom line; the leader has his eye on the horizon" (1989, p. 45).

Questions for Self-Analysis

- What is your long-range vision for your organization? Are you fully satisfied with it?
- How does this vision differ from what was present before you assumed your current position?
- What process did you follow in developing this vision?
- If you became the staff head of another nonprofit organization, how would you go about developing a vision for it?
- To what extent would you modify your vision as a result of pressures from board and staff? How do you draw the line between compromising with the views of others and maintaining your own beliefs about the organization's needs?
- What has your presence and your vision added to this organization?
- Have you challenged the status quo?

Conveying the Vision to Others

The leader's vision can have an impact only when others understand and embrace it and, most important, when it excites them to action. The best leaders, says Gardner (1990, p. 4), "put heavy emphasis on the intangibles of vision, values and motivation and understand intuitively the non-rational and unconscious elements in leader-constituent interaction."

Questions for Self-Analysis

- How did you go about communicating to others your expectations for the organization?
- What examples can you cite of how your vision for the organization was kept alive over time?
- What examples can you cite of your staff associates doing things differently because of the expectations you set forth?
- In what ways has your vision made a difference?

- What have been your greatest challenges in gaining acceptance of your vision and getting people excited by it?
- Would you convey your vision any differently if you became director of another nonprofit organization?
- What is your track record in attracting and energizing volunteers? What approaches have you found most effective?

Knowing Oneself

No one can lead effectively for long without having a thorough knowledge of self. Good leaders are adept at capitalizing on their strengths and compensating for weaknesses. According to Bennis (1989a, p. 40): "The leader never lies to himself, especially about himself, knows his flaws as well as his assets, and deals with them directly. You are your own raw material. When you know what you consist of and what you want to make of it, then you can invent yourself."

Questions for Self-Analysis

- What new things have you learned about yourself in the past several years? How have you learned them?
- What changes in your behavior or attitude would you like to make? How do you propose accomplishing this?
- Can you cite examples of your candor in assessing your strengths and weaknesses and your behavior in specific situations?
- Have you ever had any role models? What effect did they have upon you?
- Have you ever been a role model for someone else? Why or why not? Do you anticipate being a role model in the future?
- Can you cite examples of your own immaturity? If so, what do you learn from these situations?
- How often do you take stock of yourself? What is the outcome?

Standing by Your Convictions

Leaders have convictions and the strength to stand by them. This applies whether adhering to the organization's mission or projecting a vision, whether insisting on ethical practices in fund raising or dealing with staff and volunteers. Such persistence or "toughness" is not a superficial trait or a sign of rigidity. It is a basic survival skill in the nonprofit world, where most organizations are continually buffeted by conflicting forces, and compromise often is not the best course. Being consistent — in day-to-day program decisions, in contacts with funders, and in dealing with staff — is the hallmark of an organization that knows where it is going and maintains high standards in achieving its goals.

Questions for Self-Analysis

- How would people who know you well describe your ability to take a stand on a controversial issue and stick to it?
- Can you cite an example of when you took a stand on a difficult issue and stood by it in the face of pressure and criticism? What process did you go through? What was the outcome?
- How do you draw the line between compromise and the need to adhere to a principle or a decision? What is a reasonable compromise for you?
- What are examples of tough decisions you have made regarding members of your staff? What were the outcomes and how did you feel about them?
- How do you know you are right when making a difficult decision? Under what conditions would you change your position?

Taking Risks

Successful nonprofit leaders are not afraid to take calculated risks. When they fail, they learn from their mistakes rather than becoming subdued or defeated by them. Playing it "by the manual" and being immobilized by fear of failure are not the traits of a leader.

Questions for Self-Analysis

- Can you cite some risks you have taken, including examples where the outcome was uncertain, the funding was unsure, and the board and staff harbored doubts?
- What was involved in reaching the decision? Did you have any doubts as events unfolded?
- What risk might you take in the future? What would be at stake?
- Under what circumstances would you assume the directorship of a nonprofit just getting started? What assurance would you require and what abilities would you bring?
- What mistakes have you made as a result of your decisions? How did you react to these mistakes and what did you learn from them? How might those experiences affect your decisions or performance in the future?
- What would motivate you to make a decision that has a 50 percent chance of failing?

Mastering the Organization

Leaders innovate while managers merely administer and maintain, says Bennis (1989a, p. 45). Effective leaders can exploit the potential in an organization rather than be restricted by its policies and dogma. In short, the true leader believes institutions exist to serve people, not the other way around. Leaders are not bound by the status quo. They work to shape an organization in their own image, to create a vibrant culture that responds to the leader's vision and emphasizes people over procedural concerns.

Questions for Self-Analysis

- What are examples of how you changed your organization to help it better achieve its mission and adapt to your vision of its potential?

- How do you differentiate between change for its own sake and a constructive change in the status quo?
- Once changes are made, how do you maintain the new environment and how do you respond to staff members who resist change?
- If you moved on to a new job in another organization, how would you go about analyzing its culture and, if appropriate, changing it?

Before we leave the subject of leadership, two caveats are in order. First, the excellent organization is not only well led, it is also well run. Sound management provides the bedrock for leadership to flourish. The effective leader must also be an effective manager, or must delegate those responsibilities to someone else. Excellence is achieved through a combination of sound management and inspired leadership.

The second caveat is that leadership does not occur in a vacuum. In the case of the nonprofit, the leadership context includes relating to the board, staff, members, and volunteers. No matter how dynamic and inspired, the nonprofit leader can function effectively only with the support and involvement of others, especially the board chair. This key relationship is discussed in the next chapter.

Chapter Seventeen

Guidelines for Enhancing
Board Effectiveness

The third hallmark of an excellent organization is the existence of an involved and committed volunteer board, coupled with a productive and mutually satisfying relationship between the board and the chief staff officer. Each of our studies explored board dynamics, and each provides dramatic evidence that the nonprofit cannot achieve success in the absence of a well-functioning board. We now look at how a board can become most effective and how the staff executive can best work with the board and its chair.

Several books provide helpful advice from people with vast experience observing and participating in nonprofit boards. We especially recommend *Governing Boards* (Houle, 1989); *The Board Members Book* (O'Connell, 1985); *Governance Is Governance* (Dayton, 1987); and the National Center for Nonprofit Boards' *Governance Series* (especially Axelrod, 1988, and Ingram, 1988).

Functions of the Board

The members of a nonprofit board function in a governing role and as volunteers. Their prime responsibility is to ensure that the organization is well managed. However, except in small or startup operations, where there is no full-time paid staff officer, experience shows that the bord should not be involved in day-to-day management, and that the executive director should be the only staff person reporting directly to the board.

The board's major responsibilities are to:

- Determine the mission of the organization, revise it as appropriate, and ensure that programs and activities effectively carry out the mission.
- Appoint, monitor, advise, stimulate, support, compensate, and, if necessary, replace the chief staff officer.
- Review and approve long-range and annual operating plans and budgets.
- Assure that the organization's basic legal and ethical responsibilities are being fulfilled.
- Assure that adequate financial resources are secured and properly managed, review and approve periodic financial reports, and appoint independent auditors.
- Recruit, select, and elect new board members.
- Periodically appraise the board's own performance.

Enhancing the Board's Effectiveness

In the ideal board, it is the collective spirit, enthusiasm, and dedication of members that create a culture of full board involvement. There are a number of practices that, in combination, will make a volunteer board more effective.

Selecting Board Members. Over the long haul, the process for choosing members has a very significant impact on the quality and effectiveness of a nonprofit board. If the board is small, the recruitment, selection, and nomination of new members may involve the whole board, but more commonly this function is delegated to a nominating committee. Criteria for membership should be developed so that the board reflects:

- The combination of experience and skills needed for effective governance.

- Commitment to the organization, as evidenced by members' willingness to give it "their best," to attend meetings regularly, and to fulfill their dual role as both volunteer and governor.
- Diversity in age, sex, race, and any other areas appropriate to the nonprofit's constituency.

Some nonprofits consider choosing board members to be a *pro forma,* secondary function. They are depriving themselves of one of the greatest tools for board improvement.

Orienting New Board Members. A formal orientation is important, not only to educate new members about the organization and their duties, but also to convey a message about the importance of board membership. At a minimum, new members should be given descriptive material about the organization, the most recent annual report and financial audit, an organizational chart, and a job description for board members. If the board is large, an orientation session enables new trustees to get acquainted with each other before meeting the larger group.

Terms of Membership. Both research and practical experience show that is useful to designate specific terms for the board and to limit the number of terms that members serve. This helps ensure fresh blood for the organization, and it makes it easier to plan for replacing board members in a timely and thoughtful manner. Our survey of 900 nonprofit organizations (INDEPENDENT SECTOR, 1990b) found that the most effective ones, on average, limited board members to serving two three-year terms. Board chairs had an average limit of two terms of one or two years each. Staggering board terms is strongly advised to ensure continuity.

Attendance. Coming to meetings regularly is essential if a board is to function effectively. It is the only way board members can keep current on activities and issues. Repeating for absentees the points covered at previous meetings wastes time and creates frustration. The board can make best use of its time and build an *esprit de corps* only if most members consistently attend meetings. This expectation needs to be strongly emphasized when selecting new board members or asking present members to stand for reelection.

Committees. The judicious use of board committees serves two functions. It delegates operational matters below the level of the full board and thus provides a handy way to involve more board members, especially if the board is large. And it gives members a better opportunity to get to know each other, to acquire deeper knowledge of the organization, and to bring their experience and judgment to bear on vital matters.

The Board's Organizational Culture. The most crucial aspect of board effectiveness is also the most intangible: the "culture" of the board. Since the typical board meets for only a few hours each month or each quarter, it is harder to create a positive and productive environment than at the office, where staff are together perhaps forty hours a week. The factors we have already discussed — from the selection process for new members to the judicious use of board committees — play a role in determining board culture. But so, too, do the more subtle actions of the board chair and the nonprofit's executive director. A board has a positive culture when members regularly attend, when they participate actively in meetings, readily undertake volunteer assignments, and, most important of all, demonstrate enthusiasm, spirit, and dedication to the organization and its mission.

The Executive Director and the Board

The relationship between a nonprofit's board and its chief staff officer is so important that it can make or break an organization. A good working alliance can be a prime factor in success. Conversely, strong unresolved differences are probably the greatest single reason for mediocre or unsatisfactory performance. In excellent nonprofits, the board and executive director share a mutual understanding of the fundamental difference between management and governance — and who is responsible for what. Communication is frequent and honest.

An excellent way to clarify roles is to write formal job descriptions for board members and the executive director. Job descriptions should be developed with the nonprofit's own unique situation in mind. They should be reviewed carefully. And it may be helpful to discuss examples of specific actions implied by each item in the description.

In the crucial relationship between board and executive director, the findings of researchers Herman and Heimovics (1987), discussed earlier, offer important insights. Most of the executive directors they surveyed reported frequent contacts with their boards. But the most effective executives had a special kind of relationship. They made a concerted effort to involve the board actively in broad policy matters. They spent a lot of time clarifying the mutual lines of responsibility. And they worked to generate a climate of trust with the board.

Here are some specific actions an executive director can take to help nurture a positive relationship with his or her board:

- Prepare, with the board chair, a detailed agenda in advance of each meeting.
- Prepare supporting written material for major agenda items, with an emphasis on more detail, not less. Some board members, of course, will be more interested in the specifics than others. But including sufficient detailed information enables the board to make its judgments based on facts, not impressions.
- Send the agenda to board members ten days to two weeks before a meeting.
- Consult with committee chairs in advance if they are to give reports. This gives them an opportunity for input and lets them know beforehand what is expected of them.
- Make sure the physical setting of the meeting, the time allotted, and the demeanor of the board chair create an atmosphere that signals that active participation of all board members is encouraged and expected.

Communicating with individual board members between meetings is also important. Board members can often be helpful when given specific assignments within their area of interest and special competence. And doing so underscores the notion that a board member's responsibilities go beyond merely coming to meetings. Such assignments could include giving speeches or attending functions on behalf of the organization, recruiting board members, fund raising, or making personal financial contributions.

The Executive Director and the Board Chair

Perhaps no single relationship is more crucial to building an effective nonprofit organization than a strong alliance between the board chair and the chief staff officer. As head of the nonprofit's governing structure, the board chair is at the apex of responsibility for the organization. The chair has the dual role of ensuring that the nonprofit fulfills its mission and of being the number one volunteer. As Kenneth Dayton succinctly put it: The board chair "ought to love the organization more than anyone else" (1987, p. 13).

The precise duties of the nonprofit board chair may vary depending on the nature and size of the organization, but the essential responsibilities are to:

- Serve as the volunteer leader with final responsibility for the organization's health and growth.
- Create a climate that ensures the board members' active involvement in carrying out the organization's mission.
- Serve as the principal point of contact with the executive director and maintain a productive, positive relationship between the executive and the board.
- Develop with the executive director and approve the agenda for board and executive committee meetings and strategies for getting the desired results.
- Hold regular meetings with the executive director to discuss current issues and activities, evaluate progress toward objectives, and provide advice and counsel.
- Conduct an annual evaluation of the performance of the executive director, with input from the management committee or the full board.

The executive director, in contrast, should fulfill these basic responsibilities:

- Keep the board chair fully informed of program, financial, and organizational developments.
- Seek the advice and counsel of the chair on policy issues, on matters that involve other board members, and on issues that have ramifications beyond the organization.
- Solicit feedback from the chair about one's own leadership and performance.
- Develop with the chair the agenda for board and executive committee meetings and strategies for getting the desired results.
- Help the chair be aware of individual board members' views and talents.

Questions for Self-Analysis

The following questions will help you evaluate the effectiveness of your board and identify areas for possible improvement.

- How would you rate your board in terms of its commitment, involvement, and attendance at meetings?
- Has your board ever conducted a self-appraisal of its performance?
- How familiar is your board with the bylaws of your organization? When were the bylaws last reviewed or revised?
- Does the board, or a board committee, annually appraise the performance of the chief staff officer?
- Are you satisfied with the process of selecting and recruiting new board members?
- Do you feel your board is the right size for your organization?
- Is there sufficient turnover of board members to periodically bring new ideas and new perspectives into the organization?
- How would you describe the pace and quality of a typical board meeting?
- How would you rate the quality of the relationship between the chief staff officer and the board chair?
- To what extent have board members been active in fund raising and in the recruitment of new board members and other volunteers?

Chapter Eighteen

Raising Funds
and Mobilizing Volunteers

Nonprofit organizations have two types of resources—money and people. Although we will consider each separately, there is a strong relationship between the two. For one thing, the majority of voluntary nonprofits depend on contributions from individuals, either gifts or membership dues, for a sizable share of their income. In addition, INDEPENDENT SECTOR's national surveys of giving and volunteering show these two activities correlate strongly (Hodgkinson and Weitzman, 1990). People who volunteer give about three times as much as people who do not. This is not surprising. People are more likely to make monetary contributions to organizations they are personally involved with.

Monetary Resources

Our survey of nine hundred voluntary organizations revealed that the major sources of revenues for nonprofits are individual donations, government grants, allocations from United Way and

other combined campaigns, fees for services, and membership dues. Other sources of funds include grants from foundations and corporations, endowment income, and bequests. The importance of each source, of course, varies widely depending on the nature and purpose of the particular organization, and it is impossible to generalize about "the best" fund-raising technique for all situations. For example, what is most appropriate for a large art museum may produce negligible results for an urban center for troubled youth or for a group advocating the rights of the handicapped. An organization must examine a range of possible funding sources to identify those that have the greatest potential in the light of the activities and groups served by the organization.

Individuals

Data reported annually in *Giving USA* (American Association of Fund Raising Counsel, 1990) show that about 84 percent of all charitable giving comes from living individuals, 6 percent from bequests, 6 percent from independent and community foundations, and 4 percent from corporations or corporate foundations. This suggests that most nonprofits should first examine the potential for contributions from individuals.

A comprehensive description of strategies for raising funds from individuals, as well as from other sources, is found in *Securing Your Organization's Future* (Seltzer, 1987). Another useful resource is the pamphlet *Fund Raising* (O'Connell, 1987).

Questions for Self-Analysis

- Has your organization systematically identified those constituencies or groups of individuals that would be willing to support your organization if they are asked to give?
- Have you articulated the reasons your organization deserves support and what distinguishes it from other groups?
- Do you have a group of key volunteers, including board members, who are willing to make personal contributions and are willing to solicit others on a face-to-face basis? To

what extent are these activities discussed by the board and considered in the recruitment of new board members?

- Are you or have you considered becoming a membership organization with annual dues or fees? What is the potential for this type of involvement and what benefits or services could be offered?

- What is the potential for direct mail solicitation or a phonathon for your organization? Can you develop extensive lists of prospects to test the feasibility of these techniques?

- Have you explored the pros and cons of holding a fundraising event?

- Do you have board members, other volunteers, or staff members who have had fund-raising experience? If not, have you explored the possibility of outside assistance?

- Have you considered seeking a special gift or grant to support a comprehensive fund-raising or membership campaign?

Foundations

Foundations represent a potential funding source for many voluntary organizations, but with two important caveats: Foundations are the source of only 6 percent of all private giving and may receive five to ten times as many grant requests as they are able to fund. The major foundations most often concentrate on proposals for special projects or programs covering one to three years and rarely provide ongoing operating support. Independent foundations concentrate their giving in defined areas of interest and sometimes within defined geographical areas. Community foundations are found in many cities and regions, focus their giving within their locality, and are more likely to consider general support grants.

The Foundation Directory (Foundation Center, 1989a) is a good place to identify foundations interested in funding a specific activity or area of interest. It lists foundations by geographic area, the kinds of organizations they have funded, their priority giving areas, and the size of the grants they have made.

The Foundation Center has branches or collections of reference materials in many cities that can provide further in-

formation. All foundations have their own time cycles and requirements for submitting grant proposals, so it is important
to contact them directly before submitting a grant proposal.

Questions for Self-Analysis

- Have you conducted research to identify foundations that
  are most likely to be interested in the field where you seek
  funding?
- Are you embarking on a new project or proposing a feasibility study of a new program area for your organization?
- Is there a community foundation in your area? Have you
  obtained its annual report and established contact with it?
- Are you prepared to take the time and effort to prepare
  detailed grant proposals that meet the requirements of various foundations? If you receive a grant, are you prepared
  to submit periodic financial and narrative reports required
  by the foundation?
- Have you determined whether any board member or other
  key volunteer has a contact with a foundation?
- Will the project or activity terminate when the grant expires
  or, alternatively, will you have a probable source of continued funding?

Corporations

Corporations and their foundations are another potential source
of funds. The *National Directory of Corporate Giving* (Foundation
Center, 1989b) offers details on 1,500 of the largest corporate
giving programs, including the contact person in each corporation, the size of the program, and priority areas of giving.
Corporations tend to fund groups and causes in communities
where they are headquartered or have many employees. Typically,
corporate grants go to nonprofits with some tie to the company's
interests, line of business, or employees. Like independent foundations, corporations have their own individual requirements for
submitting grant requests. An initial contact should be made to
determine whether the company has interest in your organization or project and what procedures are to be followed.

Corporate contributions, unlike foundation grants, are often for general support rather than project-specific and may fund an organization year after year. This applies particularly to nonprofits located in the corporation's headquarters city, those where company employees are volunteers, or those that provide services to employees.

In addition to cash grants, corporate support can take many other forms, such as advertisements in special-event programs, donations of company products or equipment, or loaned employees to provide professional services to the nonprofit. *Resource Raising: The Role of Non-Cash Assistance in Corporate Philanthropy* (Plinio and Scanlan, 1986) gives examples of over forty different ways corporations have assisted voluntary organizations.

Questions for Self-Analysis

- Are managers or employees from a local corporation on your board or serving as volunteers? If so, have you used these contacts to approach the corporation for cash contributions or other forms of support?
- Do any local corporations have a matching gift program that matches employee gifts to qualified nonprofits?
- Does your organization provide services to corporate employees and their families and have you used this connection to approach the company for contributions?
- Have you made an inventory of your noncash needs and asked for corporate assistance in a specific area (such as holding a special event on company premises, using an office off-hours to conduct a phonathon, or asking for *pro bono* help from a company attorney)?
- Would a corporation benefit by being publicly associated with your organization or project?
- Is your organization involved with issues that may be of interest to a corporation and related to its lines of business?

Other Funding Sources

Nonprofits providing services to the public are often eligible for government support and frequently are a vehicle through which public support is channeled. Government funding, especially at the federal level, has been significantly reduced in the 1980s and is increasingly difficult to obtain. In 1987, government provided $85 billion to the nonprofit sector to provide public services, representing 26 percent of the total revenue of all voluntary nonprofits in the nation (Hodgkinson and Weitzman, 1989, p. 37). Descriptions of steps involved in obtaining government support, supplemented by lists of additional sources of information, are found in Chapter 15 of *Securing Your Organization's Future* (Seltzer, 1987) and in *Getting Funded: A Complete Guide to Proposal Writing* (Hall, 1988).

Many organizations are in a position to generate income from fees for their services or from business activities related to the organization's charitable purpose. Typical examples include nonprofit hospitals or clinics charging fees for services, private nonprofit colleges and universities collecting tuition, or museum stores. *The Nonprofit Entrepreneur* (Skloot, 1988) contains how-to-do-it strategies and examples of organizations that have generated income while carrying out their charitable purpose.

Another interesting example is provided by the Citizens' Scholarship Foundation of America. For a number of years, CSFA's sole activity was organizing and supporting local Dollars for Scholars chapters that raised funds in their communities to provide college scholarships for local young people. The concept was a sound one and CSFA eventually formed a number of chapters, but was unable to establish sufficient sources of consistent funding and periodically faced financial crises. Then the organization happened upon an opportunity to exploit its experience in establishing and administering scholarship programs. The opportunity came in 1975 in the form of a chance contact with a corporation that wished to establish and fund a scholarship program for the sons and daughters of its employees. CSFA tailored a program to the needs of the Toro Company and annually serves as an independent administrator to select scholarship recipients from a pool of applicants and pay out scholarship funds provided by Toro. In the ensuring years, CSFA expanded this type of service to over three hundred corporations and now administers $20 million in annual scholarships.

Fees received for administering the corporate programs have placed the organization on a sound financial footing and, supplemented by other grant funds, have provided for the formation and technical support of 505 Dollars for Scholars chapters in 33 states that raise over $4 million a year in scholarship aid for local young people.

Another source of funds for many organizations is support received from an annual federated drive such as a local United Way, Black United Fund, Combined Health Appeal, or Arts Council. These campaigns rely heavily on workplace solicitation of company and government employees, supplemented by direct corporate contributions. The federated or umbrella agency makes allocations of the collected funds to local organizations by conducting a comprehensive evaluation of the programs, management systems, and financial condition of each organization. The majority of organizations supported by the federated drives are involved in the delivery of health and social services to the public. Chapter 17 of *Securing Your Organization's Future* (Seltzer, 1987) provides information on how to obtain support from a federated organization.

Volunteers

What would the nonprofit world be without volunteers? They annually provide over 15 billion hours of volunteer time equivalent to $150 billion worth of services. They are docents at the museum, drivers of Meals on Wheels, readers for the blind, assistants at a neighborhood health clinic, telethon operators, tutors and mentors and Little League coaches. The list is endless.

But in spite of this level of activity, many organizations have not fully tapped their potential for volunteers. Just as nonprofits differ from one another with respect to the appropriateness of different fund-raising techniques, so do they vary in ways they can most effectively use and motivate volunteers. The challenge is to define appropriate jobs for volunteers and to recruit those who can identify with the organization and have the skills and motivation to do the job. And the link between volunteering and fund raising should not be overlooked; about 13 percent of all formal volunteer activity is in this area.

In the process of selecting organizations to receive its Excellence in Management awards, the Beatrice Foundation evaluated several hundred nonprofit organizations over the past five years. From this experience, the foundation identified a series of "keys to management excellence." One of these is "A clear understanding that volunteers are plentiful, if recruited, trained and managed well, but that this precious resource cannot be taken for granted; skilled volunteer coordinators may be the key" (Beatrice Foundation, 1989, p. 11).

For some excellent how-to tips on recruiting, screening, motivating, and empowering volunteers, we suggest *Essential Volunteer Management* (McCurley and Lynch, 1989). Timely examples of corporate volunteer programs are found in *A New Competitive Edge: Volunteers from the Workplace* (Vizza, Allen, and Keller, 1986).

Questions for Self-Analysis

- How satisfied are you with the current quality and quantity of volunteer involvement in your organization? What have been the trends in this regard over the past several years?
- Have you made a list of ways in which volunteers could play a more meaningful role in your organization? Have you developed brief job descriptions for specific volunteer positions?
- Have you developed a plan for recruiting and selecting volunteers, with emphasis on matching a volunteer's desires, expertise, and time commitment with the needs of your organization?
- Have you contacted a local volunteer center or similar agency that recruits and places volunteers?
- Have you contacted local corporations to learn if they have programs to encourage volunteering by their employees and retirees?
- Have you considered using committees below the board level as a way of actively involving more volunteers?
- Do you have a formal program for recognizing volunteer service? Do you have examples of volunteers who have moved up to positions on your board?

- Have your chief staff officer and board chair given a high priority to the effective use of volunteers?
- If you can use a number of volunteers, have you considered hiring a part-time or full-time volunteer coordinator to concentrate in this area?

Although the raising of financial and volunteer resources may not capture the imagination to the same extent as the other hallmarks of excellence, no nonprofit can claim the "excellent" label without it. Resource raising must be a continuing priority of the chief executive and the board chair as they continually search for the fund-raising and volunteer-involvement strategies that will enable the organization to fulfill its mission and provide the continuity required for high-quality programs.

Planning for Excellence

We have described a wide range of techniques for applying the four hallmarks of excellence: mission as the guiding force, presence of a true leader, existence of a dynamic board, and the ability to attract resources. But where to begin? It is not possible for the average organization to embark on a number of improvement steps simultaneously. The most appropriate actions must be selected and priorities established.

A useful guide to setting priorities is provided by examining the current growth stage of the organization. In the same way that institutions differ from one another in nature and purpose, they also vary in age and, more important, in their position on the growth curve of nonprofits. In this concluding chapter we examine the characteristics of three stages in the growth of voluntary organizations (startup, growth, maturity) and focus on ways you can tailor improvement strategies to your own setting. We will discuss the key challenges an organization faces at each stage and suggest ways to conduct an internal self-evaluation and capitalize on the perspective provided by outside resources.

Stage One: Startup

The first organizational phase typically is characterized by a small group of volunteers, or perhaps a highly motivated individual, responding to a cause, issue, or problem. The initial goals tend to be subjective and the group may lack the expertise needed to form a nonprofit organization. The greatest assets are the active involvement of volunteers with a common purpose, the existence of a pervading "can-do" entrepreneurial spirit, and possibly the presence of a charismatic founder.

The greatest challenge facing the startup organization is overcoming problems attendant to its small size. The Beatrice Foundation Awards for Excellence program evaluated several hundred nonprofits over the years and made awards to organizations in three size categories, based on annual revenues. They had this to say about the smallest organizations, those with annual revenues under $250,000: "It has become increasingly difficult for the smallest groups to succeed at management excellence. Their struggle to serve constituents can consume them to the point of survival, rather than excellence. Over the years, it has become clear that some invisible threshold must be crossed before small groups can even begin to consider management excellence" (Beatrice Foundation, 1989, pg. 11).

The challenges, then, for the fledgling organization revolve around those activities that bring it stability and enable it to grow to a size where it can concentrate on the quality of its programs and services, rather than on its sheer survival. The challenges are:

- For the founders to agree upon and articulate a shared vision for the organization in the form of a mission statement.
- To set modest but specific goals for the first year or two of operation, develop a plan for reaching the goals, and adhere to the plan.
- To evaluate potential resources for fund raising and obtain the best possible assistance to develop a fund-raising plan.
- To enlarge the volunteer base by concentrating on people who identify with the goals of the organization and who can help it in specific ways.

- To formalize its structure by developing bylaws, filing for incorporation in the home state, and establishing its tax-exempt status with the U.S. Internal Revenue Service.
- To establish and maintain an accurate accounting system.

Stage Two: Growth

The growth stage is attained when the organization has survived the startup period, achieved some stability in funding, and reached the level where a full-time executive director and other staff members are employed. The board may be enlarged, bringing with it diversity and resources appropriate for the growing organization. The feeling pervades that further expansion in funding, membership, and programs is achievable and staff and board are motivated in that direction. At the same time, the group has learned that the road to success is not straight and well paved; adherence to sound management practices is accompanied by trial-and-error learning as obstacles are overcome. The board faces the fact that its role has changed because it is not doing everything itself, and the executive director builds a staff and learns to work effectively with the board.

A principal challenge is keeping alive the spirit and momentum initiated by the founders and achieving expansion without distorting the original mission. Other challenges include:

- Developing a plan for maintaining the funding base after startup grants and initial gifts run out.
- Expanding or diversifying the board to include people who are willing and able to help the organization as it grows.
- Building a membership base or other core of volunteers and financial supporters.
- Developing a formal annual plan with measurable goals and objectives, supplemented by a long-range plan extending three to five years in the future.

Organizations can fail and go out of existence in either of the first two stages of growth, so the ultimate objective is to successfully meet the challenges encountered in those stages to be able to move to the third stage. Those fortunate enough to find themselves in stage three are still faced with the challenge of attaining and preserving excellence in an ever-changing world.

Stage Three: Maturity

The mature organization may still be growing, but it has reached a degree of stability and self-sufficiency that enables it to devote more time and energy to evaluating and improving itself. It is likely to have become more institutionalized and bureaucratic as it grows in size and complexity. It has identified and been successful with its funding sources and has a well-developed planning and control system. Generally, the mature organization has developed a credible track record and is in a good position to attract givers and volunteers.

At the same time, the mature organization is not without substantial challenges. The very size and current stability that are the envy of other nonprofits can provide an illusory sense of security that prevents the organization from adapting to changes in the world around it and maintaining its fund-raising momentum. Corporate dinosaurs headed for extinction are not restricted to the for-profit world!

The mature organization must:

- Keep a large, prestigious board fully involved and committed.
- Ensure that the organization does not become so staff driven that the board becomes a tool of the chief staff officer, with volunteers relegated to mundane tasks.
- Maintain a keen ability to be aware of and respond to external changes that affect the organization's ability to carry out its mission. For example, the Girl Scouts and Big Brothers/Big Sisters reacted to demographic and geographic changes by developing inner-city programs and encouraging participation of young people of all races.
- Pay attention to the needs and problems of a larger staff, including their desire to be part of the decision-making process.

- Recognize the need for self-renewal among staff and board members, including bringing new persons and new ideas on the scene.

Evaluating Your Organization

The best way to identify strategies for improvement is to conduct an evaluation of the organization — how well is it doing and how can it do better? We will consider a straightforward process to help an organization evaluate itself and then explore potential outside sources of assistance that provide insights not available from people close to the institution.

At the outset, you must determine what is to be evaluated and how. This is best done within a simple planning framework established at the start of each year. In that process, it is important that the people involved — chief staff officer, board members, and staff — participate in and reach consensus on the need for a plan and the course to follow. The planning framework consists of four steps:

1. Developing the organization's mission statement or reviewing the existing mission statement.
2. Developing specific goals for the coming year that carry out the mission.
3. Listing activities required to meet the goals.
4. Listing criteria to be used to measure results — establishing yardsticks for determining whether or not the goals are achieved by year-end.

Completing these steps at the start of the planning period sets the stage for carrying out the evaluation at the end of the year. This can be a simple process; the active involvement of staff and board is more important than elaborate details. The plan serves as a guide during the year as well as the framework for year-end evaluation.

There are several advantages to conducting an annual self-evaluation:

- It provides a basis for taking timely corrective action.
- It lets the board know what is going on.
- It is useful in informing current funders how their money is being spent and providing prospective funders with solid information about how well the organization is operating.
- For larger organizations, a parallel evaluation process can be applied to each department or program area to provide more details on strengths and areas for improvement and to let department heads know how they are doing.

A second aspect of self-evaluation concerns a nonprofit's performance in fulfilling its responsibilities to the public as a trustee of the charitable funds it receives. Comprehensive checklists of ethical and fiduciary standards are provided by the National Charities Information Bureau (1988) and the Council of Better Business Bureaus (1982). A fuller exploration of ethical issues facing nonprofits is found in *Obedience to the Unenforceable: Ethics and the Nation's Voluntary and Philanthropic Community* (INDEPENDENT SECTOR, 1990a). That publication presents the recommendations of INDEPENDENT SECTOR's Committee on Values and Ethics. The committee is composed of nonprofit leaders, legal scholars, journalists, consumer and social advocates, and representatives of higher education and religion. The Committee recommends that all organizations in the voluntary sector adopt an organizational credo and conduct an internal ethics review every year. It also recommends that larger organizations develop a supportive set of codes or standards, involve all of their constituencies in the process, and infuse the process and the documents into the culture of the organization (1990a, p. 5).

Assistance from Outside the Organization

Although periodic self-evaluation is the essential first ingredient, the perspective provided by qualified outsiders is also useful. The Beatrice Awards Program concluded that one of the keys to management excellence was "an organization's willingness to use outsider advisors from professional management consulting firms, pro bono technical advisors or peer nonprofit organizations whose mission is to serve the sector" (Beatrice Foundation, 1989, p. 11).

A wide range of resources is available to nonprofits seeking outside advice or assistance. Beatrice Awards applicants in the Chicago area have used these resources: volunteers from the Executive Service Corps (retired executives with specialized experience in such fields as marketing, accounting, planning, human resources, and general management), United Way staff specialists, the Support Center (a technical assistance group serving nonprofits in a number of cities), Business Volunteers of the Arts, the local grantmakers' forum, the consulting group of a major accounting firm, and faculty members from a local university. O'Connell points out in *Evaluating Results* (1988a) that additional outside resources for groups affiliated with a national organization include members from the national staff or a team of peers from other chapters of the organization. For those without a national organization, O'Connell suggests assembling a local team of several of the best staff directors and most experienced board volunteers from other nonprofits in the community.

In instances where volunteer or *pro bono* assistance is not available or appropriate, some organizations have obtained grant support for professional consultants. There is increasing recognition among foundations that evaluating organizational effectiveness is a key to helping nonprofits improve themselves. This, in turn, helps ensure that basic support grants are being well spent.

The skilled outside evaluator brings an objectivity and perspective that the insider lacks. Consultants often find that insiders may not be identifying and defining the problem appropriately or may be asking the wrong questions. This is often the case when the problem involves relationships among individuals rather than technical, programmatic, or financial matters. The insider is at a particular disadvantage when he or she is part of the problem and may not recognize it or be willing to admit it.

Another invaluable use of a well-qualified consultant is to obtain information and opinions from people outside the organization. Frequently numerical data are not available or relevant to evaluate activities or programs and a mail survey will not yield the most meaningful information. A trained outsider is more likely to elicit candid and complete information from respondents through interviews or focus-group discussions and can more objectively analyze the resulting information so it will be most useful to the organization.

For example, INDEPENDENT SECTOR wished to determine how well its government relations program had informed, educated, and influenced the federal government in specific recent legislative and regulatory matters, and how successfully it had established and maintained effective working relationships with Capitol Hill and government agencies. A consultant worked with the government relations staff to frame questions and then conducted face-to-face and telephone interviews with members of Congress and their staffs, members of the press who follow the nonprofit sector, and other knowledgeable outside observers. The consultant then analyzed and interpreted the resulting information.

In summary, key evaluation activities can be carried out effectively by the staff and board, but the perspective and skills of persons outside the organization are often helpful. The current growth phase of the organization also influences the nature of the evaluation process and the questions the institution should ask itself.

A Final Word

In this volume, we have sought to distill the findings of recent research studies of key factors contributing to the excellence of voluntary nonprofit organizations. We have relied on real-life examples to substantiate the findings, have examined ten very different organizations in some depth, and have proposed actions nonprofits can take to achieve excellence.

This is not an operational handbook for the startup or day-to-day administration of nonprofits, but a volume to encourage nonprofit staffs and volunteers to raise their organization from a level of practical competence to true excellence. In the process, we have emphasized four caveats:

1. Organizational excellence must be built on a foundation of sound management practices.
2. No organization is perfect, and there are always opportunities for further improvement.
3. No single prescription is equally applicable to all nonprofits; each must find the improvement strategies that best fit its circumstances.
4. The road to excellence and maturity is not smooth; learning from mistakes is as important as going by the book.

We hope the principles, techniques, resources, and examples will help your organization strive for excellence. The next steps are up to you!

References

American Association of Fund Raising Counsel. *Giving USA*. New York: American Association of Fund Raising Counsel Trust for Philanthropy, 1990.

Axelrod, N. R. *The Chief Executive's Role in Developing the Nonprofit Board*. Washington, D.C.: National Center for Nonprofit Boards, 1988.

Beatrice Foundation. *Awards for Excellence — 1989 Observations*. Chicago: Beatrice Foundation, 1989.

Bennis, W. *On Becoming a Leader*. Reading, Mass.: Addison-Wesley, 1989a.

Bennis, W. *Why Leaders Can't Lead*. San Francisco: Jossey-Bass, 1989b.

Bennis, W., and Nanus, B. *Leaders: The Strategies for Taking Charge*. New York: Harper & Row, 1985.

Campbell, J., Bownas, D., Peterson, N., and Dunnette, M. *The Measurement of Organizational Effectiveness*. NTIS No. AD-786-462. San Diego: Navy Personnel Research and Development Center, 1974.

Carver, J. *Boards That Make a Difference.* San Francisco: Jossey-Bass, 1990.

Council of Better Business Bureaus. *Standards for Charitable Solicitations.* Arlington, Va.: Council of Better Business Bureaus, 1982.

Dalton, D., and others. "Organizational Structure and Performance: A Critical Review." *Academy of Management Review,* 1980, *5,* 49–64.

Dayton, K. N. *Governance Is Governance.* Washington, D.C.: INDEPENDENT SECTOR, 1987.

Dunlop, J. J. *Leading the Association: Striking the Right Balance Between Staff and Volunteers.* Washington, D.C.: Foundation of the American Society of Association Executives, 1989.

Foundation Center. *The Foundation Directory.* New York: The Foundation Center, 1989a.

Foundation Center. *National Director of Corporate Giving.* New York: The Foundation Center, 1989b.

Foundation of the American Society of Association Executives. *The Personal Equation: A Critical Look at Executive Competency in Associations.* Washington, D.C.: ASAE Publications, 1989.

Gardner, J. W. *On Leadership.* New York: Free Press, 1990.

Grantsmanship Center. *Whole Nonprofit Catalog.* Los Angeles: Grantsmanship Center, 1990.

Hall, M. S. *Getting Funded: A Complete Guide to Proposal Writing.* Portland, Or.: Continuing Education Publications, Portland State University, 1988.

Herman, R. D., and Heimovics, R. D. "Effective Managers of Nonprofit Organizations." In *1987 Spring Research Forum Working Papers.* Washington, D.C.: INDEPENDENT SECTOR, 1987.

Hodgkinson, V. A., and Weitzman, M. S. *Dimensions of the Independent Sector.* Washington, D.C.: INDEPENDENT SECTOR, 1989.

Hodgkinson, V. A., and Weitzman, M. S. *Giving and Volunteering in the United States.* Washington, D.C.: INDEPENDENT SECTOR, 1990.

Houle, C. O. *Governing Boards: Their Nature and Nurture.* San Francisco: Jossey-Bass, 1989.

INDEPENDENT SECTOR. *Aiming High on a Small Budget: Executive Searches and the Nonprofit Sector.* Washington, D.C.: INDEPENDENT SECTOR, 1986.

INDEPENDENT SECTOR. *Obedience to the Unenforceable: Ethics and the Nations' Voluntary and Philanthropic Community.* Washington, D.C.: INDEPENDENT SECTOR, 1990a.

INDEPENDENT SECTOR. *Self-Perceptions of Effectiveness: A Survey of Nonprofit Voluntary Organizations.* Washington, D.C.: INDEPENDENT SECTOR, 1990b.

Ingram, R. T. *Ten Basic Responsibilities of Nonprofit Boards.* Washington, D.C.: National Center for Nonprofit Boards, 1988.

Kouzes, J. M., and Posner, B. Z. *The Leadership Challenge: How to Get Extraordinary Things Done in Organizations.* San Francisco: Jossey-Bass, 1987.

McCurley, S., and Lynch, R. *Essential Volunteer Management.* Downers Grove, Ill.: VM Systems and Heritage Arts Publishing, 1989.

National Assembly of National Voluntary Health and Social Welfare Organizations. *A Study in Excellence: Management in the Nonprofit Human Services.* Washington, D.C.: The National Assembly, 1989.

National Charities Information Bureau. *Standards in Philanthropy.* New York: National Charities Information Bureau, 1988.

O'Connell, B. "The Search for Excellence: Lessons for Philanthropy." Speech to Annual Meeting of the New York Regional Association of Grantmakers, 1984.

O'Connell, B. *The Board Member's Book: Making a Difference in Voluntary Organizations.* New York: The Foundation Center, 1985.

O'Connell, B. *Fund Raising.* Nonprofit Management Series No. 7. Washington, D.C.: INDEPENDENT SECTOR, 1987.

O'Connell, B. *Evaluating Results.* Nonprofit Management Series No. 9. Washington, D.C.: INDEPENDENT SECTOR, 1988a.

O'Connell, B. *The Roles and Relationships of the Chief Volunteer and the Chief Staff Officers, Board and Staff: Who Does What?* Nonprofit Management Series No. 5. Washington, D.C.: INDEPENDENT SECTOR, 1988b.

Plinio, A., and Scanlan, J. *Resource Raising: The Role of Non-Cash Assistance in Corporate Philanthropy.* Washington, D.C.: INDEPENDENT SECTOR, 1986.

Schein, E. H. *Organizational Culture and Leadership.* San Francisco: Jossey-Bass, 1985.

Schein, E. H. "Organizational Culture." *American Psychologist,* 1990, *45,* 109–119.

Seltzer, M. *Securing Your Organization's Future: A Complete Guide to Fundraising Strategies.* New York: The Foundation Center, 1987.

Skloot, E. *The Nonprofit Entrepreneur: Creating Ventures to Earn Income.* New York: The Foundation Center, 1988.

Vizza, C., Allen, K., and Keller, S. *A New Competitive Edge: Volunteers from the Workplace.* Arlington, Va.: VOLUNTEER: The National Center, 1986.

Index

658.048
K67

83603

LINCOLN CHRISTIAN COLLEGE AND SEMINARY